Essays in Real Estate Research

Volume 18

Series Editors

Nico B. Rottke, Frankfurt, Germany

Jan Mutl, Wiesbaden, Germany

Die Reihe „Essays in Real Estate Research", herausgegeben von Professor Dr. Nico B. Rottke FRICS und Professor Jan Mutl, Ph.D. umfasst aktuelle Forschungsarbeiten der Promovenden der Lehrstühle und Professuren des Real Estate Management Institutes der EBS Business School. Forschungs- und Lehrschwerpunkte des Institutes bilden die interdisziplinären Aspekte der Immobilientransaktion sowie die nachhaltige Wertschöpfungskette im Immobilienlebenszyklus. Die Kapitalmärkte werden als essenzieller Bestandteil der Entwicklung der Immobilienmärkte aufgefasst. Die in der Regel empirischen Studien betrachten transaktions- und kapitalmarktnahe Themenbereiche aus dem Blickwinkel der institutionellen Immobiliengewerbe- und -wohnungswirtschaft, wie bspw. Finanzierung, Kapitalmarktstruktur, Investition, Risikomanagement, Bewertung, Ökonomie oder Portfoliomanagement, aber auch angewandte Themen wie Corporate Real Estate Management, Projektentwicklung oder Unternehmensführung. Die ersten 11 Bände der Reihe erschienen bis 2014 auch im Immobilien Manager Verlag, Köln.

The series "Essays in Real Estate Research", published by Professor Dr. Nico B. Rottke FRICS and Professor Jan Mutl, Ph.D., includes current research work of doctoral students at the chairs and professorships of the Real Estate Management Institute of EBS Business School. The research and teaching focus of the Institute constitutes the interdisciplinary aspects of real estate transactions as well as the sustainable value creation chain within the real estate life cycle. The capital markets are regarded as essential components of the development of the real estate markets. The mostly empirical studies consider transactional as well as capital market topicsfrom the point of view of the institutional commercial and residential real estate industry, such as finance, capital market structure, investment, risk management, valuation, economics or portfolio management, but also applied topics such as corporate real estate management, real estate development, or leadership issues in the property industry. The first 11 volumes of the series appeared up until 2014 in Immobilien Manager Publishing, Cologne, as well.

More information about this series at http://www.springer.com/series/13911

Jan de Graaff

Essays on the Impact of Urban (Dis-)Amenities on the German Real Estate Market

With a Foreword by Prof. Dr. Nico B. Rottke

Springer Gabler

Jan de Graaff
Bonn, Germany

Doctoral Thesis, EBS Business School, EBS Universität für Wirtschaft und Recht, Wiesbaden, Germany, 2019

ISSN 2570-2246 ISSN 2570-2254 (electronic)
Essays in Real Estate Research
ISBN 978-3-658-31622-8 ISBN 978-3-658-31623-5 (eBook)
https://doi.org/10.1007/978-3-658-31623-5

This Springer Gabler imprint is published by the registered company Springer Fachmedien Wiesbaden GmbH part of Springer Nature.
The registered company address is: Abraham-Lincoln-Str. 46, 65189 Wiesbaden, Germany

Foreword

The research study “Impact of Urban (Dis-)Amenities on Residential Real Estate Prices in Germany” by Dr. Jan de Graaff deals with the relationship between location factors and residential property prices in major German cities.

The study employs the concept of “urban amenities” – roughly describing urban infrastructure; urban amenities; urban comfort. The theoretical basis assumes that people increasingly see cities as centres of consumption and want to live in places that offer the best conditions to consume. The “urban amenities” are consumed by the inhabitants of a city or town, i.e. they provide the inhabitants with the comfort of consumption. In theory, therefore, locations with a high (or low) number of urban amenities (or disamenities) should be in greater (or lesser) demand and the urban (dis)amenities should, thus, contribute to price formation.

“Urban amenities” can have not only positive but also negative demand effects meaning that the presence of certain location factors have a negative impact on prices, as the location becomes less attractive and thus the possibility of consumption or its quality decreases. It is important to note that especially large cities show negative side effects due to population density and the associated social frictions. The state regularly tries to reduce these side effects through political measures to keep the location attractive. These measures result in the presence or absence of certain “urban amenities” and therefore influence the demand for housing in this location.

This work does not so much focus on the theoretical assessment of urban infrastructure but builds on existing theoretical and empirical constructs of urban infrastructure, whose classification follows the Anglo-Saxon literature. The central question is whether the findings of the evaluation of individual “urban amenities” from the Anglo-Saxon literature are transferable to other countries and markets, or whether there are different price implications to those in the known literature. In comparison to the USA, the U.K. or meanwhile also China, continental European literature offers very few empirical studies that follow the concept of “urban amenities”. Therefore, this study provides important empirical findings that contribute to and expand the discussion of the above-described context.

The work is solidly based and breaks new ground in the important area of the economic assessment of real estate in relation to the subject of the study, Germany. Methodologically, the work is particularly innovative, especially in chapter 2. The work consists cumulatively of three individual services with a great potential for individual publication in internationally recognized economic or real estate journals. I therefore wish the work the recognition in research and practice that it fully deserves in an increasingly important field of research.

I wish the author Mr. de Graaff himself all the best for his future. I have come to know him as a highly motivated, always "grounded" young man who, as a team player, advanced the Real Estate Management Institute at EBS Business School and played a decisive role in shaping the team. He deserves the special honour of being the last doctoral student I was allowed to supervise for the first time before I completed the chapter on science myself, which I have been applying in practice for several years now.

Schlangenbad Professor Dr. Nico B. Rottke

Preface

The decision to pursue a doctorate and write a dissertation is an easy one. Depending on whom you ask you will get encouraging or discouraging answers to that question. Once you start being a doctoral student you try to push knowledge further and are enthusiastically about the many interesting paths you can take in achieving your goal. Yet, the further you are in the process of writing your thesis, the better you understand how complex and difficult the world can be. This experience humbles you and teaches you to be precise and that things might not be as they appear to be.

The topic I chose is not a straightforward choice but was driven by the fascination about cities. Trying to understand how they work and evolve is a very relevant and interesting topic that I wanted to contribute to. I also suppose I made my life unnecessarily difficult by trying to write about German cities as it turned out that one of the most difficult things was the lousy data availability and data quality in Germany. I pursued many ideas but was always pushed back by that limitation. I am proud that it worked out, nevertheless.

Being a doctoral student is a great but also exhausting time. Great because you have the flexibility and time like never again to dive deep into a topic of that interests you personally without too much distraction of daily business or short-term goals. Exhausting because you gradually realize how much work and how many redundancies are involved in completing a presentable academic contribution. The willingness to constantly review your own work and thoughts is what academia demands of you. The most important character traits you need are the intrinsic motivation to spend 4 years writing a dissertation and the power of endurance to finish it. However, the utmost important thing every doctoral student depends on is help. Help from your supervisors, fellow doctoral students, institutions, and fellow researchers in your field.

A couple of people played a key role in achieving this. My first and second supervisors Prof. Dr. Nico B. Rottke and Prof. Dr. Joachim Zietz. Prof. Rottke as the guiding spirit that put me in the position of writing a dissertation and provided among his expertise in the field a lot of moral support throughout the years and especially towards the end. Prof. Zietz for the endless expertise, numerous skype sessions and showing me always a way out of many dead ends during my research. Without him, it would have been absolutely hopeless. Heiko as my co-author and the many critics at numerous academic conferences. Christopher, Allyn, Sebastian, Aga, Max P., Markus, Stephan, and a few more as good friends that I made during that time. Naturally, my parents' and brother's support both financially and morally and their patience with me was fundamentally important.

Wiesbaden Dr. Jan de Graaff

Table of Content

List of Figures

List of Tables

List of Abbreviations

ACI	Average Consistency Index
AHP	Analytic Hierarchy Process
AIK	Akaike Information Criterion
ANP	Analytic Network Process
AR	Auto Regressive (Term)
BAMF	Bundesamt für Migration und Flüchtlinge (Federal Agency for Migration and Refugees)
BART	Bay Area Rapid Transit
CBD	Central Business District
CEO	Chief Executive Officer
CI	Consistency Index
CR	Consistency Ratio
DPD	Dynamic Panel Data
ECB	European Central Bank
EU	European Union
FE	Fixed-Effects
GMM	Generalized Method of Moments
IV	Instrumental Variable
LAU	Local Administrative Unit
LOR	Lebensorientierte Räume (Living Oriented Spaces)

MCDM	Multi-Criteria Decion Making
OECD	Organisation for Economic Co-operation and Development
OLS	Ordinary Least Squares
SBIC	Schwartz Bayesian Information criterion
UK	United Kingdom
UN	United Nations
US	United States (of America)
VIF	Variance Inflation Factor

1 Introduction

Economists attribute the existence of cities traditionally to *scale effects* and agglomeration effects. The first effect is better known as *economies of scale*, which means that firms can produce more efficiently on large scaled factories and sites. In general, scale effects are important drivers of growth because an increasing scalability will allow firms to produce more efficiently and therefore grow faster. The second effect relates the existence of cities to the more productive collaboration between firms due to a better availability of input factors, such as raw materials, labour, and capital. An isolated firm will have higher costs in obtaining its input factors than firms that are located in large agglomerations. On the contrary, a firm's input as well as output factors can be easier obtained and distributed in agglomerations than if the firm resides in a remote place. Furthermore, transportation costs decrease in agglomerations as distances to customers, suppliers, as well as workers are shorter. Hence, firms will cluster in areas where they find the best supply of input factors and where the transportation to the local markets is most efficient. One way to look at cities is therefore being an efficient centre of production that allows for faster growth of businesses. More productive businesses will also attract the necessary workforce and will cause higher paying jobs in agglomerations.

The focus on firms' location choices as the driver for agglomerations has been discussed in urban economics for decades. The central question is if economies of scale and agglomeration economy suffice to explain the existence of cities. Diamond and Tolley (1982) argue that the amenity concept provides a more comprehensive framework to explain the behaviour of land values, urban density, as well as household and business location choices within cities. Following previous works, Glaeser, Kolko and Saiz (2001) more recently introduced the concept of the "Consumer City" meaning that cities are not only efficient centres of production, but will increasingly be centres of efficient consumptions. With increasing wealth, people tend to be critical about the location they live at and will chose locations with the highest quality of living instead of choosing the location only on the availability of the best jobs. Of course, eventually the best jobs will be there where the people are, and vice versa. Yet, the question remains what is there first. Furthermore, in service sectors, people tend to find suitable jobs easier and can move at lower costs, because jobs depend more on the em-

J. de Graaff, *Essays on the Impact of Urban (Dis-)Amenities on the German Real Estate Market*, Essays in Real Estate Research 18,
https://doi.org/10.1007/978-3-658-31623-5_1

ployee's skills and less on the production facilities. A car manufacturer, for example, cannot move its production site in the short run. An employee must therefore move to the specific location of the site to work there. Service jobs are easier transferred from one location to another, which implies that employees in service sectors are more mobile and choose their location more freely. The means of the digitalization and automatization will further enable people to choose their location depending on their personal preference without having to move because the workplace demands it. Therefore, consumption of urban amenities will become increasingly important in the future and will determine the location choice of households, and in the consequence of firms.

Analysing the quality of locations is an important part of real estate economics with practical implications for developers, investors, and homeowners. A deeper understanding of the quality of a location will eventually allow to anticipate demand, which allows investors and consumers to make better decisions. The concept of locational and urban amenities is generally applied to evaluate the quality of locations. Amenities are goods that are consumed by households and firms at a specific location. Moreover, these goods cannot be moved easily and are bound to that specific location. The consumption of amenities will therefore only be possible at a specific location, which enables people to improve their consumption of amenities by moving to locations with higher amenity density. Assuming that households and firms seek to maximize the consumption of urban amenities, the amenity concept can explain several aspects of urban and real estate economics, such as urban land values, patterns of urban density, as well as the locations of households and business within and around cities as the movement of firms and households towards the highest amenity areas will drive the demand for these areas (Diamond & Tolley, 1982). An increase in demand will result in higher prices in the short-run due to the low elasticity of supply of real estate.

A categorization of urban amenities as consumption goods is provided by Glaeser et al. (2001). They propose four categories of urban amenities covering most of the determinants for the attractiveness of a location. The four categories are *localised goods and services*, *aesthetics and physical surrounding*, *public services*, and *speed in terms of transportation*. As stated above, the common attribute of all amenities is that they are local goods that depend on the location and cannot be substituted easily. For example, goods, such as washing machines, are produced at one place and then distributed to the buyer anywhere in the world, which makes them a non-local and moveable good. A restaurant or a bar, however, is only at one location and difficult to move. Surely, a franchise would come close to reproducing restaurants at multiple places, but the restaurant with its social value, the kind waiters, the good atmosphere will differ from one franchise restaurant to another. Clark (2004) provides comprehensive evidence that people tend to move towards localised goods and services. However, Clark (2004) identifies differences in amenity preference among the demographic cohorts. For example, college students prefer constructed amenities, such as bars, pubs, and museums whereas elderly people move towards areas with higher natural amenities. Möller (2013) also identifies the tendency of internet firms to move towards higher density localised goods. These firms are willing to pay a premium to be located in areas where the density of bars, pub, cultural facilities are higher. Glaeser and Gottlieb (2006) find similar results for art museums, restaurants, and concert halls. Hence, households and firms demand localised goods and services and are willing to pay premiums for areas with a high density of such goods.

Aesthetics and physical surrounding are the second category and also unique goods from an economic perspective. A pleasant view, the proximity to a river, to the mountains, or a special architecture are examples of local characteristics of a specific location that cannot be substituted. Empirical research shows that especially natural amenities play a vital role in determining the quality of locations. Anderson and West (2006), for example, show that open spaces in urban areas have a positive impact on real estate prices. Mahan (1997) provides further evidence that the proximity to wetlands in Portland, Oregon drives housing prices. Households are willing to pay higher prices the closer they are located to lakes, parks, and green open spaces. Gibbons, Mourato, and Mendes (2014) find a similar relationship for England. Their very comprehensive study with over 1 million transactions shows a positive value of natural amenities on housing prices. Furthermore, Glaeser et al. (2001) argue that architectural beautiful cities, such as San Francisco, developed better on a macroeconomic level than other less appealing cities. Other empirical studies show that the proximity to heritage buildings can have positive price effects (Ahlfeldt & Mastro, 2012), or that appealing architecture can drive office rents. Vandell & Lane (1989) and Gat (1998) find such evidence for office rents in Boston, Cambridge, and Tel Aviv.

The third group of amenities are the public services, which refer to various governmental services that local municipalities offer to make cities liveable. The interest of many researchers on public services resides in the fact that findings can be translated into public policy recommendations because the responsibility for providing these services lies within the government. The two most commonly studied subjects in this field are education and safety. The quality of education, or in other words schools, plays an important role in household location choice. In a literature review, Nguyen-Hoang and Yinger (2011) outline the empirical evidence between school quality and housing prices published since 1999. They conclude that on average prices rise by just below 4% for one standard deviation increase in student test scores. Hence, people are willing to pay a price premium to allow their children to attend schools that promise better school grades. Most studies analyse US data sets, but evidence is also found for the UK, France, and Norway.

Another important public service subject is safety, which can be understood quite broadly, but is usually connected to police work and the maintenance of a low crime rate. Compared to rural areas, cities are usually considered to be crime hot spots (Ellen & O'Regan, 2010). The renewed interest in cities is often attributed to sharp crime declines during the 1990s. Glaeser and Gottlieb (2006) argue that the decrease in big city crime allowed urban residents to enjoy and consume urban amenities more freely since the threat of victimization decreased during those years. Furthermore, Cullen and Levitt (1999) report that one additional reported crime per capita results in a 1% decrease in population. Hence, crime has an impact on people's willingness to live at a specific location, which eventually should influence prices through the change in demand. Thus, the acknowledging the impact of crime seems very relevant for policy makers and will be analysed in Chapter 4 in detail.

Besides education and safety, the government provides many other public services that focus on the avoidance of disamenities to the population. Pollution and noise are among the most relevant ones. Riker and Henning (1967) were one of the first to evaluate the effect of air pollution on residential house prices. They identified significant negative effects of air pollution on housing values using hedonic regression techniques. Furthermore, Nelson (1979) found evidence that airport noise pollution affects housing prices by -0.50% for every decibel increase in airport noise. Libscomb (2003), on the contrary, finds that people from smaller cities value the proximity to an airport higher than potential disamenities from noise pollution.

Transportation is the fourth category in the framework of urban amenities by Glaeser et al. (2001). More specifically, *speed* is the aspect that is achieved by a good transportation infrastructure. The better the transportation infrastructure, the faster one gets from A to B. The distance usually matters in terms of time rather than in terms of kilometres. Past empirical works focus on the effects of newly constructed infrastructure projects, such as railways or highways, and on commuting times. A prominent study by Cervero and Landis (1997) showed that the Bay Area Rapid Transit (BART) in San Francisco had a positive impact on urban growth. Especially downtown San Francisco became more accessible and allowed the office market to prosper. However, San Francisco did not profit from the construction evenly, but enhanced the development in areas that did already quite well. Glaeser, Kahn and Rappaport (2008) come to a different conclusion for other US cities. They show that poorer people use public transportation because they cannot afford other modes of transportation. They suggest that this could explain the segregation of poor and wealthy people within cities. On the one hand, poor and wealthy people both value proximity to their places of interest, but on the other hand poor need to live close to public transportation to reach those places. Wealthier people will have more choices in terms of transportation and will usually prefer to move by car and not by public transportation. Hence, poorer people will select locations close to cheaper modes of transportation that allow them to move. Yet, Orazem, and Otto (2011) support the argument of traditional agglomeration economists that households trade commuting costs against higher housing prices in urban areas. The better the public infrastructure, the more viable it is for the households to live in suburbs or rural areas that are connected to that infrastructure.

The attractiveness of a location is likely to be measured by the level of housing prices against the background that people tend to move towards more attractive parts of a city. As mentioned above, a demand shift for housing will increase prices in the short run because of the relatively low elasticity of supply. The stock of housing is fixed in the short run because a) the production of houses is time consuming, and b) the land for construction in certain areas cannot be multiplied. Due to this fixed supply of housing, an increase in demand should increase housing prices. Therefore, housing prices serve as a good indicator for the attractiveness of an area as they should implicitly reflect all the information that people have about a specific property and location that makes the area attractive to them. Most papers use this assumption and conduct hedonic modelling studies that uses property prices as the dependent variable and the variables of interest, such as the urban amenities, as the explanatory variable. This approach allows to determine to what extent the price is determined by the respective urban amenity.

1.1 Motivation and Problem Definition

The goal of this thesis is twofold: further investigate the impact of urban amenities and disamenities on residential housing prices and household location choice in Germany, and add empirical evidence to the discussion. The regional focus is on Germany because empirical research is scarce with regards to the relationship of urban amenities and residential housing prices. Furthermore, Germany experienced interesting developments in recent years with regards to people's increased movement towards cities resulting in a residential real estate boom. Furthermore, the public debate in Germany knew four major topics during the past years: mass-migration, criminality, housing prices, and climate change. Climate change might be a future topic for household location decisions on a macro level, but will be disregarded in the scope of this thesis because of the lacking relevance for Germany. However, migration, crime and increasing housing prices are relevant short-term to medium-term topics that are worth to be further investigated.

Firstly, very little is known about the German households' location choices. Möller (2013) provides empirical evidence that localised goods and services, and transportation drives firms' location choices in Berlin. However, empirical evidence about the drivers of households' location choices is lacking. Regression techniques require comprehensive data sets that are often difficult to obtain for Germany. Especially when estimating large geographical areas, price data for Germany is rare. Hence, this thesis uses a different approach and uses a multi-criteria decision-making (MCDM) methodology used in management decision making processes to survey German households about their location choice preferences. This stated-choice methodology is to some extend unconventional in the urban amenity literature, but aims at contributing a new perspective of approaching the topic, while building on previous empirical papers that investigated this topic conventionally.

Secondly, the mass-migration of people from the Levante, Sub-Sahara Africa and the Maghreb states since 2015, which is often referred to as the "refugee crisis", caused a controversy among policymakers and the public about the consequences for the housing markets and on society as a whole. As chapter 3 illustrates, approximately 2 million people had to find accommodation in the brief period of two years. Surely, many migrants were offered special refugee camps after arrival but after the process of granting asylum they were eligible to social housing throughout the country. In the context of urban amenities (or disamenities), the question arises if an increase in migrants from different parts of the world will have an impact on the original population and on the housing prices.

Thirdly, migration is not only but also associated with driving crime. Phrasing it differently, the fear of increasing crime is tied to an increase in migrants. However, criminologists know that crime is more a matter of education and wealth. Wealthier neighbourhoods provide fewer violent crime exposure (Tita, Petras, & Greenbaum, 2006). Based on fact that most migrants and especially refugees belong to the poorer parts of society, higher crime rates are more likely among these groups (Baier & Pfeiffer, 2007). Additionally, men and especially young men are proportionally more criminal than women, which means that large amounts of young men will drive crime. The migration statistics shows that most refugees that arrived between 2014 and 2015 are young men under the age of 30. Hence, the question is whether increasing crime is an issue in our cities and whether it influences prices in a measurable way.

1.2 Course of Investigation

This thesis comprises of three separate research papers that represent one chapter each in this thesis. Chapter 2 investigates the location choice decisions of German households by applying Analytical Hierarchy Process (AHP) methodology. The idea is not to implicitly measure the factors through the analysis of housing prices, but to explicitly ask the consumers of the urban amenities to rank a set of location criteria. After introducing the topic, section 2.2 explains the AHP in detail and provides a small example to ensure the reader understands the methodology, since it is not very common in urban economics. Section 2.3 outlines the study design, sample selection, and explains the structure of the questionnaire. Henceforth, section 2.4 provides the results of the ranking and the preferences of different subsamples of the survey. Finally, a brief discussion compares the obtained results to previous findings.

The 3rd chapter investigates the role of migration on residential housing prices in Berlin, Germany. The question is if migration has a) an impact on the housing situation of the original residents, b) if the origin of migrants has different impacts on housing prices, and c) if migration works as an exogeneous shock when the relative increase of immigrants is high. After providing insights about the topic in general, section 3.2 outlines the immigration history of Germany as a whole, and Berlin in particular. Section 3.3 outlines the data set. Section 3.4 includes the methodology, which is divided into two parts: Part I deals with the impact of migration in general on housing prices in Berlin and the movement of the original population; Part II uses an innovative difference-in-difference approach to investigate immigration shocks by including dummy variables that depend on the relative change of immigrants in a certain area. The result section 3.5 is also divided into two parts similar to the methodology section 3.4. The discussion in section 3.6 compares the findings with previous research and discusses the robustness of the estimations.

The third paper deals with the impact of crime on residential prices in Hamburg, Germany. The paper follows established empirical strategies and takes on the methodological issues of endogeneity and autocorrelation. Section 4.2 outlines the existing literature on crime and housing prices. Section 4.3 illustrates the data set. The empirical strategy in section 4.4 involves an outline of the strategy to deal with the methodological difficulties. The results are briefly presented in section 4.5 before section 4.6 includes a comprehensive in-depth discussion of the results and potential methodological improvements. The discussion leads to the formulation of 5 propositions for further researchers to obtain more robust results in future research. The chapter ends with a conclusion in section 4.8.

2 Analysing the Location Choice Preference: An AHP Approach for Germany

2.1 Introduction

Household location choices are important determinants for the structure of urban agglomerations. They influence economic growth, social structure, infrastructure investments, social and spatial segregation, and the level of urbanity. In urban economics, the modelling and understanding of household location choice is therefore an important topic to provide guidelines for urban planners, developers, and policy makers on what to focus in their decision-making.

Location choices drive the demand for real estate property. They depend, in turn, on a combination of quantitative and qualitative factors that households attach value to. In real estate development and urban planning, the anticipation of demand is crucial to develop suitable properties and shape the cities according to people's preferences. In urban economics, cities are considered as efficient centres of production where people would want to live because they find higher paying jobs. However, research over the past two decades shows that there appears to be a shift in people's mind toward viewing urban spaces as a consumption good (Glaeser et al., 2001). The idea behind the city as a consumption good is that people consume the accessible urban amenities and chose their place to live according to their needs. As people become wealthier and are more likely employed in the service sector, they become more flexible in choosing their preferred location, because service industries tend to be more diversified than manufacturing industries and it is easier to find a comparable job in alternative locations. Hence, cities and developers need to provide space that suits the inhabitants' preferences to stay attractive to current and future citizens. Furthermore, they compete with other cities for inhabitants, which is crucial for cities to stay prosperous and maintain an elevated level of urbanity.

Different techniques exist to identify the preferences of city dwellers from an operational point of view. They can be divided into the application of regression techniques to identify implicitly the choice people made or by surveying their actual preferences. The first group uses hedonic regression techniques to construct price indices by regressing transaction data with various structural or envi-

J. de Graaff, *Essays on the Impact of Urban (Dis-)Amenities on the German Real Estate Market*, Essays in Real Estate Research 18,
https://doi.org/10.1007/978-3-658-31623-5_2

ronmental characteristics over time. This methodology assumes real estate prices to be a value function of the set of collected characteristics and their parameters.

The second group explicitly tries to identify preferences by surveying decision makers, such as households or individuals. Discrete choice modelling is one of the best-established methodologies to identify the overall utility a location has for the decision maker. A decision maker chooses the alternative with the highest utility from a set of mutually exclusive alternatives. For example, the researcher provides three locations of three cities and asks the decision maker to rank them according to their preferences. The researcher cannot identify all attributes that the decision maker faced and he or she cannot distinguish among the attributes. The researcher provides a set of structural and location characteristics which are the basis for the respondent to judge the utility. However, the researcher does not catch why the respondent values one higher than the other.

The Analytical Hierarchy Process (AHP) represents an alternative to discrete choice modelling. AHP is a multi-attribute decision-making approach developed to model complex management decision-making problems (Saaty, 1977). The approach uses *pairwise* comparisons of the various attributes that are relevant for making the decision. In contrast to the discrete choice models, AHP catches the exact ranking of attributes and allows a deeper analysis of the relevance of attributes among decision-makers. The knowledge obtained by AHP about the relative weighting of the attributes may be used during the investment and developing process to assess the quality of a location. Furthermore, urban planners and policy makers could use the information to improve urban environments and to set priorities appropriately in the face of limited resources. This paper provides an example of such an analysis. In particular, it will determine the relative importance of urban amenities by conducting a survey among a representative sample of German residents applying the AHP methodology.

The paper is organised as follows. First, the existing literature regarding urban amenities and AHP will be reviewed. The second step consists of the identification of relevant urban amenities that ought to be surveyed. Thirdly, the methodology of AHP will be described. Fourthly, the sample selection strategy will be outlined, and the sample data will be described. Fifthly, the results are presented and analysed with respect to demographic and social factors. The paper ends with some concluding remarks and suggestions for further research.

2.2 Modelling Location Choice Preferences with AHP

AHP is a multi-criteria decision modelling (MADM) method for complex decision-making problems. Saaty (1977, 1986) invented AHP and applied it throughout his career on decision-making problems in different fields. Unlike classical multi-attribute modelling approaches that explicitly model utility functions, AHP derives relative priorities from relative measures of two criteria. The basic principle consists of a respondent weighting two criteria against each other to derive their relative importance. The comparisons result in a comparison matrix, which finally results in a normalized priority vector representing a hierarchy among all criteria. The advantage of AHP is that it is much easier to compare two alternatives in complex decision environments instead of grasping the relative importance of many alternatives at the same time. As AHP uses a strict hierarchical process, true to its name, it can best be understood by following the 5 steps that make up AHP. In the following, an example will show how AHP works and how a decision is made. It is important to note that AHP may be structured in many different ways, so that the following example only represents the basic setup that includes the essential elements.

Every AHP starts with the problem definition. It is important to clearly state the problem and make sure that this problem is solvable by AHP. Furthermore, the problem definition is necessary to determine the scope of the decision problem. As shown later, the number of alternatives plays a key role for the feasibility of AHP, which is why a clear problem definition is essential to make the decision problem neither unnecessarily complex nor overly simplistic.

The second step involves the structuring of the decision-making problem. AHP represents a special case of the more general Analytical Network Process (ANP) (Saaty, 1999). What is special about AHP is that the decision-making problem is structured in layers that represent a hierarchy. Unlike AHP, ANP does structure the decision-making problem as an à priori hierarchy but treats every level of the hierarchy as equal. In principal, the decision-making problem is structured into three layers: the goal, the criteria, and the alternatives. The goal is the problem to be solved, the criteria are the relevant elements that differentiate the alternatives from each other. The alternatives represent the possible outcomes that the decision maker wants to choose from. Furthermore, AHP allows to group certain criteria into categories under the assumption that the categories do not interfere with each other for the whole of the decision-making problem.

The following example provides a simple illustration of AHP. If the goal is to choose the CEO for a company, Figure 1 shows the decision-making tree. The first level represents the goal, which in this example will be the choosing of a CEO. The second layer represents the relevant criteria for hiring the CEO. In this case work experience, education, charisma, and age are the only criteria to play a role. The weighting of the four criteria is unknown and will be determined by AHP. The third layer contains the three candidates that will be eligible as CEO. Technically, AHP allows one to add layers and to deal with more complex decision-making problems. For example, the criteria could be divided into sub-criteria to use more refined information. To keep the illustration simple, the example sticks to one layer of criteria.

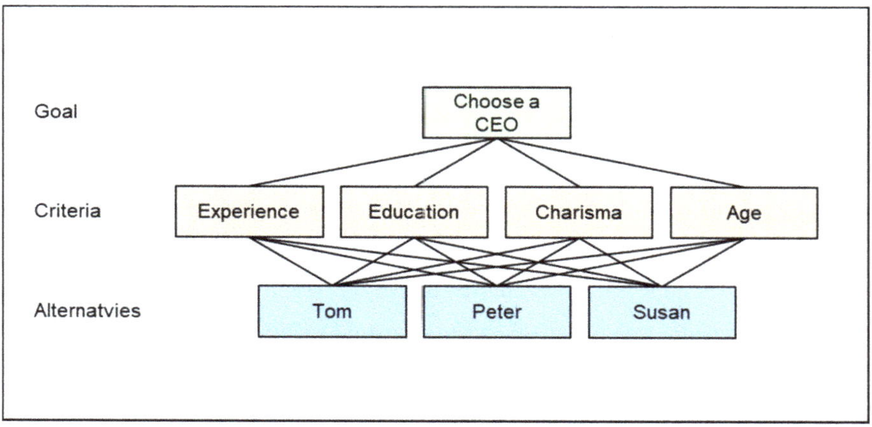

Figure 1) Example Structure of an AHP to Choose a CEO. Source: Own Illustration.

	Experience	Education	Charisma	Age
Experience	1			
Education		1		
Charisma			1	
Age				1

Figure 2) Pairwise Comparison Matrix of the Criteria to Choose a CEO. Source: Own Illustration.

The third step consists of setting up the pairwise comparison matrix for the four criteria to determine their relative importance. The matrix shows each criterion on the y and x-Axis. In the next step, all criteria will be ranked against each other on a specific scale, which will be explained below. The relative importance of the same criterion is always 1. The matrix will be symmetric, which means that the respondent must only compare two criteria once. The comparison of *Education* and *Charisma* will have the reciprocal value of the comparison of *Charisma* and *Education.* Hence, the number of comparisons is determined by the number of criteria and is calculated as

$$N = \frac{n*(n-1)}{2}, \tag{1}$$

where N is the number of comparisons and n is the number of criteria. In the example, six comparisons are necessary, which represents the triangular block under or above the diagonal. For a detailed mathematical description of the *eigenvalue* problem, see Appendix A.

The fourth step is the actual comparison of the criteria. The comparison is conducted along the typical AHP 9-point scale (Mu & Making, 2015). Table 1 exhibits a 9-point scale that is derived both empirically as well as theoretically. The scale is well established for AHP in practice and is derived from the Weber-

Fechner-Law[1]. Fechner derived from Weber's work that the relationship between a stimulus and its perception is logarithmic. This means that if the stimulus, for example, triples (3x1) the perception will only double (1+1) and if it triples again (3x3x1) it will only add one to the perception (1+1+1). The Weber-Fechner-Law is formalized as

$$M = k \log \frac{S}{S_0} \quad (2)$$

where M is the sensation, k is a constant, S is the stimulus and S_0 is the threshold stimulus. From this relationship any noticeable stimulus increases geometrically, but the response to it increases only arithmetically. Hence, the response scale must have consecutive numbers to grasp the arithmetical response.

Saaty and Vargas (2001) further argue that, in general, humans can qualitatively divide their responses to stimuli in three categories: high, medium low. Furthermore, humans can refine this division by subdividing each of the three categories into high, medium, and low again. Saaty and Vargas (2001) exemplify the choice of the scale by extending the scale to 1-721, which leads to higher inconsistencies because the brains of humans can manage only a lower number of objects (Saaty & Vargas, 2001, p. 35). From an operational point of view, two criteria will always be presented as counterparts with the scale from 9 to 1 to 9. The respondent will then rate on this scale, which of the two criteria is more important than the other. For example, criterion A is 3 times more important than criterion B, which results in a 3 on the 1-9 scale. Therefore, criterion B is 1/3 as important as criterion A, which represents the reciprocal relationship.

---

1 Ernest Heinrich Weber (1795-1878) and Gustav Theodor Fechner (1801-1887) both worked on stimulus, response, and ratio scale research. Especially Weber developed the theory of a minimum stimulus size that allows people to judge differences. He found that people were able to distinguish between two weights of 20g and 21g but not between 20g and 20.5g. He concluded that the minimum size of a stimulus for people to notice a difference between two things depends on the minimum difference relative to the size of the things. Fechner formalized this and mathematically derived the minimum stimulus size necessary for people to make judgments (Saaty & Vargas, 2013, p. 305).

Table 1) 9-point AHP Scale. Source: Saaty and Vargas (2001, p. 6)

Intensity of importance	Definition	Explanation
1	Equal Importance	Two activities contribute equally to the objective
2	Weak	
3	Moderate Importance	Experience and judgment slightly favour one activity over another
4	Moderate Plus	
5	Strong Importance	Experience and judgment strongly favour one activity over another
6	Strong Plus	
7	Very Strong or demonstrated importance	An activity is favoured very strongly over another; its dominance demonstrated in practice
8	Very, very strong	
9	Extreme Importance	The evidence favouring one activity over another is of the highest possible affirmation
Reciprocals of above	if $W_{ij} = k$, then $W_{ji} = k^{-1}$	

This will become clearer with an example. The pairwise comparison will be done for the lower triangle using the fundamental scale of AHP. The results could look as Figure 3 shows:

	Experience	Education	Charisma	Age
Experience	1	1	4	7
Education	1	1	3	4
Charisma	1/4	1/3	1	2
Age	1/7	1/4	½	1

Figure 3) Comparison Matrix Including Pairwise Comparisons Using the 1-9 Scale. Source: Own Illustration.

In the example, *Education* is rated as equally important as *Experience*; *Charisma* is only ¼ as important as *Experience* and so on. This is done for all pairs of criteria, which will result in the comparison matrix of Figure 3. In decision-problems with multiple categories or hierarchies, this is done for every category of criteria or hierarchy. In the end, normalized eigenvectors will allow to calculate relative weights of all criteria, based on the relative weights of the hierarchy above.

The fifth step is the synthesis and calculation of the priorities. As explained above, this is done by calculating the eigenvector of the matrix. The mathematical procedure to solve the eigenvalue problem is always the same for any application and is well described by Nguyen (2014, p. 40); it can also be found in the publications by Saaty (1986, 2001). Due to an inconsistent choice[2], the final weights of the four categories are calculated by raising the matrix to an arbitrarily large power and dividing the sum of each row by the sum of the entries in the matrix. The final normalized weights of the criteria are:

Table 2) Results of the Example of the AHP for 4 Criteria with a Single Hierarchy. Source: Own Illustration.

Experience	44.5%
Education	36.1%
Charisma	12.3%
Age	7.1%

To decide, which candidate is to be preferred, one must repeat the procedure for every criterion and rate the candidates with regard to this criterion. This means that for *Experience* one comparison matrix will be set up that includes the three candidates. The three candidates are then judged with respect to each criterion using the fundamental 9-point AHP scale against each other. To obtain a ranking of all three candidates, the results of candidate priorities are weighted according to the weights obtained above. Figure 4 illustrates the pairwise comparison matrices of every candidate eligible to become CEO with respect to each criterion. The weight vectors of the comparison matrices in Figure 4 are then multiplied by the relative importance (weight vector) of the criteria. Equation 3 represents the

2 Inconsistent judgments are likely to occur, because respondents will only judge two criteria at a time and might violate the importance of an earlier or later judgement of one criterion to a third one. For example if A is twice as important as B and B is three times more important than C, then A must be six times more important than C. A different judgment than 6 would lead to an inconsistent judgment. However, for group decision making the inconsistencies disappear as Bender et al. (1997) have shown because the inconsistent matrices are normally distributed and are likely to cancel each other out. Furthermore, Mazurek and Perzina (2017) show that inconsistency will always be present in AHP but will not affect the weighting of the criteria for group decisions.

final calculation of the weights multiplying the relative importance of the criteria with the weight vectors of the candidates from Figure 4:

$$S_w = \begin{bmatrix} 0.135 & 0.610 & 0.061 & 0.600 \\ 0.367 & 0.225 & 0.333 & 0.300 \\ 0.498 & 0.166 & 0.606 & 0.100 \end{bmatrix} \begin{bmatrix} 0.445 \\ 0.361 \\ 0.123 \\ 0.071 \end{bmatrix} = \begin{bmatrix} 0.330 \\ 0.307 \\ 0.363 \end{bmatrix} \quad (3)$$

The interpretation is that Susan is the best suited CEO with a score of 0.363 against Tom with 0.330 and Peter with 0.307.

An important aspect is the consistency of choices. It is likely that the decision-maker will choose inconsistently. Especially in complex decision-models with many criteria, the chance that the matrix is inconsistent is high. As stated above, the error is measured by the difference between the maximum eigenvalue of the consistent matrix and the maximum eigenvalue of the inconsistent one.

$$CR = \frac{CI}{ACI} \quad (4)$$

Where *CR* is the consistency ratio and the consistency index (*CI*) is defined as,

$$CI = \frac{\lambda_{max} - n}{n - 1} \quad (5)$$

The ACI is the average consistency index of randomly generated reciprocal matrices using the fundamental AHP scale. In general, a constituency ratio of less than 0.1 is accepted as sufficiently close to a consistent matrix (Bender, Din, Hoesli, & Laakso, 1999; Saaty & Vargas, 2001). However, Bender et al. (1997, p. 510) showed that for survey data the consistency is of minor importance as the results of samples with only consistent answers and samples with all answers will show the same results. The reason is that the inconsistencies are normally distributed and cancel each other out if the sample size is sufficiently large. As the sample is quite large for our group analyses, the consistency measures can likely be neglected.

Experience

	Tom	Peter	Susan	Weights
Tom	1	1/2	1/5	13.5%
Peter	2	1	1	36.7%
Susan	5	1	1	49.8%

Education

	Tom	Peter	Susan	Weights
Tom	1	2	5	61.0%
Peter	½	1	1	22.5%
Susan	1/5	1	1	16.6%

Charisma

	Tom	Peter	Susan	Weights
Tom	1	1/6	1/9	6.1%
Peter	6	1	1/2	33.3%
Susan	9	2	1	60.6%

Age

	Tom	Peter	Susan	Weights
Tom	1	2	6	60.0%
Peter	½	1	3	30.0%
Susan	1/6	1/3	1	10.0%

Figure 4) Comparison of the Alternatives with Respect to the Criteria. Source: Own Illustration.

A last feature of AHP is group decision making, which will be relevant for the empirical part of this chapter. Until now, the underlying assumption is that a single person undertakes the pairwise comparisons. However, it is also possible to aggregate individual decisions to group decisions. In short, the geometric mean of all individual decisions is the appropriate way to aggregate individual to group decisions (Saaty & Vargas, 2013, p. 23).

2.3 Study Design

The empirical part will use the AHP methodology to identify the relative importance of location criteria based on data from a representative survey. Several studies have been conducted along these lines, in each case applying the same methodology, but using different criteria and surveying different samples. Saaty (1986) used the AHP methodology in his earlier works to identify the most liveable city in the US. Applying AHP methodology, he had 6 respondents rate quantifiable location criteria of cities against each other. The criteria he used come close the what hedonic modelling identifies as urban amenities. The criteria involved were: Climate, Housing, Healthcare, Crime, Transportation, Education, Arts, Recreation, and Economics. More recently, Kauko (2006, 2007) conducted expert interviews with 17 and 22 participants and 6 criteria with a geographical focus. He interviewed real estate experts from Budapest (Kauko, 2006), Helsinki, and Randstad in Holland (Kauko, 2007) to assess a number of location criteria using AHP. The goal was to identify what made a particular location attractive for consumers. In the Helsinki and Randstad cases, the criteria were *External Accessibility*, *Internal Accessibility*, *Service Infrastructure*, *Social Factors*, *Physical Environment*, and *Municipality*. He derived the criteria from the choice literature discussed earlier and the logistic and hedonic regression literature, without, however, referencing the origins of the criteria. The hierarchy that is employed is simplistic in the sense that it only has one level of criteria; it does not include a third level of hierarchy that would usually involve the alternatives to be chosen from. In the small example in Section 2.2, this would be the three people eligible to become CEO. However, it is reasonable from an operational point of view to keep the hierarchy as simple as possible, because the more complex the hierarchy the more difficult it gets to obtain consistent and useful responses.

Few studies with AHP and survey data use location quality criteria. Bender, Din, Favarger, Hoesli and Laakso (1997) and Bender, Din, Hoesli, and Laakso (Bender et al., 1999) conducted such surveys for households in the Geneva area. Bender et al. (1997) use eight criteria to survey 153 households in Geneva.[3] The criteria were quietness of an area, public transportation, distance to the city centre, good view, social standing of the area, distance to schools, distance to commercial facilities, and distance to green area. The second study (Bender et al., 1999) put the focus on geographical areas within Geneva and divided the sample into four areas. Furthermore, the sample selection was not among households but

3 From today's perspective this number is very satisfactory as they conducted this survey in 1994 by sending out paper-based questionnaires to 850 households with a total response rate of 22.7%.

professionals, such as advertising professionals, officers of professional associations, real estate brokers, engineers, financial advisors, lawyers, and medical professionals. They sent out 1,800 questionnaires to the different groups of professionals and received back 444 responses, which were unevenly distributed among the professional groups. The criteria differed from the first survey because of the focus on commercial real estate users. In this second study, quietness of an area, proximity to public parking, to local transportation, to long-distance transportation, proximity to the city centre and to mail and bank locations were used.[4] Compared to the earlier study, a multiplicative scale was used instead of a linear scale, which ensures that extreme ratings have less of an impact on the final weights, which helps to reduce inconsistencies (Bender et al., 1999).

Following Kauko (2006, 2007) and Bender et al. (Bender et al., 1997, 1999) this study surveys a sample of households about their location choice preferences. Based on a representative sample of households, the idea is to extract locational preferences from how households rate location criteria that have proven to be important in other empirical research, such as hedonic modelling. As the survey also collects socio-demographic variables on the households that reveal their locational preferences, it will be possible to create different subsamples and investigate differences in preference between different social groups. The next two sections identify the relevant criteria and outline the questionnaire layout as well as the sample selection.

2.3.1 Identification of Criteria

Most previous studies derive the criteria from previous research and use only a few categories of urban amenities. This paper will emphasize the choice of criteria. Instead of using a single hierarchy, two hierarchies are employed. This will allow us to gain a more detailed picture of the importance of location attributes. Our starting point is the categorization by Edward Glaeser (2001), who argues

4 The last two criteria show that this study is from the 1990s. In today's world the distance to the post office or the bank would not be considered important but would be substituted by other criteria.

that urban amenities that determine location quality can be grouped into four categories: Localised Goods and Services, Aesthetics and Physical Setting, Public Services, and Speed in terms of Transportation. These four categories are similar to the categories of Kauko (2006, 2007) and Bender et al. (Bender et al., 1997, 1999). Limiting the analysis to just four categories makes it possible to use more sub-criteria, yet still keep the complexity manageable.

For each category, the literature provides empirical findings on its influence on location quality and housing prices[5]. Overall, 52 attributes are identified that show significant relationships to housing prices[6]. Rating 52 attributes in four categories is not be feasible in a survey design. For that reason, they are grouped into 17 subcategories. A complete list of all 51 criteria with their corresponding sources can be found in Appendix A.

As shown in Figure 5, each of the four categories may have a different number of criteria. The objective for survey respondents is to choose the location for a new apartment under the current financial constraints. The question to be asked is always the same and only differs for the two criteria that are rated against each other. The questionnaire was pretested among 20 students form Mannheim University, which resulted in a further refinement of the criteria.

5 Housing prices represent as a function of endogenous and exogeneous attributes of the property or area. Hence, housing prices are the accepted measure of location quality, which is why research that dealt with housing prices was considered to identify the location attributes.

6 By no means is this list complete as the hedonic modelling literature is extensive. Yet, the list represents an extensive collection of attributes. Furthermore, this list was presented at the Annual Conference of the American Real Estate Society in Bonita Springs, Florida 2016 and was then refined and commented by the audience.

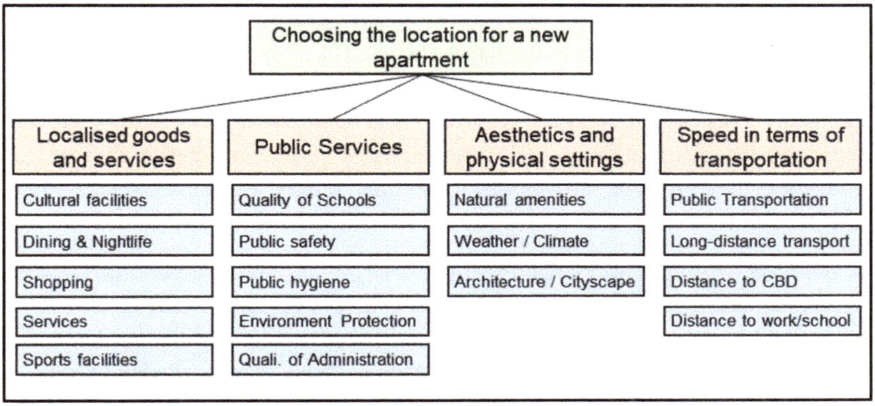

Figure 5) Representation of the Hierarchy of the Decision-Making Problem "Choosing the Location for a new Apartment". Source: Own Illustration.

2.3.2 *Questionnaire and Sample Selection*

The survey was conducted as an online questionnaire. It was sent to 2,232 individuals by a professional research service provider[7]. The objective was to receive at least 666 completed surveys to fulfil the requirement for a representative sample. The minimum sample size is derived as follows. The population eligible to choose an apartment is defined as all people older than 15 years living in Germany, which are around 68 million people. Allowing for an error margin of 5% and a confidence interval of 99%, the minimum sample size to represent a population of 68 million is 666. The sample size can be calculated with the following formula:

$$S = (\frac{z^2 * p(1-p)}{e^2})/(1 + \left(\frac{z^2 * p(1-p)}{e^2 N}\right)) \qquad (6)$$

7 Respondi AG is a Cologne based firm that provides access to their panel of 30.000 German households that covers different socio-economic groups.

where N = is the population size, e the margin of error and z- the respective z-score obtained from standard deviation tables. The sample is selected by quotas that are determined by age, gender, education and in what federal state the respondent lives. The quotas are derived from the federal statistical office and represent the distribution in 2018. Appendix A shows the distribution of age, education, federal state, and gender. The final sample contains 683 completed and useful questionnaires.

A question of some importance is how to analyse the results given that the preferences of one group may not be the same as those of another. Different methods are available to analyse the preferences of different social classes. Social classes are determined by various demographic factors, such as age, education, and income (Barreto, Frasure-Yokley, Vargas, & Wong, 2018). Other frameworks, such as the Sinus-milieus[8], divide societies into 10 target milieus according to a variety of indicators related to demographics, social class, or political preferences. The drawback to identifying which milieu a person belongs to is the need for an extensive questionnaire, which is would be beyond the scope of this study (Sinus Institut, 2019). A useful alternative is to classify along demographic cohorts, better known as the Silent Generation, Baby-Boomer, Generation X, Millennials (Generation Y), and Generation Z (Dimock, 2018). The advantage lies in the ease of classification as only age is needed. Furthermore, sociological research (Mitchell, 2008) suggests that that members of these cohorts tend to have homogeneous preferences regarding life and ethics, which derive from some common experience in growing up during a particular time.

The generations represent demographic cohorts for Western societies and vary in the birth years depending on the country's development. In general, the US cohorts start a couple of years earlier than the European cohorts, which might be due to the cultural leadership of the US after the second world war (Meyer, 2010; Mitchell, 2008). The definitions for the generations this paper follows are based on the German birth cohorts and differ slightly from the typical US definitions.

8 SINUS-Milieus are a framework conducted by the SINUS-Institute that divides society into 11 milieus based on their social status. The SINUS-Institute conducts market research and analyses the social properties of societies (Arnold et al., 2017, p. 153).

The cohorts are determined by the birth year and are categorized according to the of the respondents at the time of answering the questionnaire end of 2018. The *silent generation* includes everybody older than 65 years. The baby-boomers range from age 50 to 65, which represents the years with the highest birth rates. Generation X includes middle aged people that are between 35 and 50 years old when answering the questionnaire. The millennials or Generation Y are between 20 and 35 years old. Generation Z includes all those younger than 20 years at the time of the questionnaire.

Although the division of the population into cohorts is accepted in public debate and among scholars, some researchers criticize the concept as too superficial (Dietz, Enste, & Eyerund, 2016). The criticism relies on the fact that very similar results typically emerge for different cohorts unless one controls for education, income and milieu. Dietz, Enste and Eyerund (2016) conclude, in particular, that there is no such thing as a Generation-Y; other factors, such as education, determine instead the observed differences in preferences and behaviour. However, we suggest that age and, therefore age cohorts, may very well play a role for preferences regarding location; younger individuals tend to prefer other locations than older ones. Furthermore, Glaeser et al. (2001) argue that cities become increasingly attractive because they are centres of consumption. In this context, market research regularly shows that there are substantial differences in consumption behaviour by age (de Sombre, 2013). Furthermore, people tend to change their consumption behaviour over their personal lifecycle as Wakabayashi and Hewings (2002) have shown for Japan. Hence, there are reasonable arguments to suggest that the generational framework suitable for the analysis of preferences in the context of urban amenities. For that reason, this paper will stick to the generation clustering.

Groupings other than by age are likely of interest for our study. Geographical categorization, for example, may show relevant differences between cities and the countryside, between Eastern and Western Germany, and across the different federal states. The former division of Germany into East and West may be of particular interest in this respect, as forced differences in consumption behaviour lasted a long time. Even many years after unification, the Eastern part still lags behind the Western part economically. Hence, many economic issues or needs may differ between the Eastern and Western parts of Germany. For example, unemployment is higher on average in the Eastern states with an unemployment rate of 6.3% in 2019 compared to only of 4.3% the Western states (Statista, 2019).

The questionnaire was distributed in German to German[9] residents only; it can be found in Appendix A. Quota sampling was used to identify the individuals to which to send questionnaires. The quota sampling was done according to the first four questions; it would exclude a participant from proceeding if one quota had been filled already.[10] The other questions regarding demographics and social status were collected to be able to analyse the results more coherently. The questionnaire is based on the assumption that the respondent is looking for a new apartment given his or her current financial constraints. The question asked is the same for all criteria and reads as follows:

"In terms of the location choice for your new apartment, which of the two factors is more important to you?"

A small box with explanations above each question allowed respondents to check in case they were unsure about the meaning of a criterion. Each hierarchical layer presented in Figure 5 involved one separate page of comparisons. The first set of comparisons involved the four categories, the second set of comparisons involved the five criteria of the category *Localised Goods and Services*, next *Natural Amenities*, then *Public Services* and finally *Transportation*. The average response time to complete the survey was 8:35 minutes.

---

9 The questionnaire was translated by a committee of 4 PhD students that have a TOEFL iBT score of at least 90 as they were enrolled at EBS University's PhD program, which requires that score.

10 Quota sampling works by limiting the sample to a certain combinations of the respondents' demographic properties. For example, men and women should be equally represented in a sample of 500. Then a quota is imposed that only 250 men and 250 women can complete the survey. If 250 men already answered, the 251st man to answer will not be included in the final sample but will be excluded. The questionnaire remains open for answering until all quotas are completed.

2.4 Results

Priorities of the Full Sample

The final weight vector for the full sample, which includes all 683 answers, is depicted in Table 3. The normalized weight vector is the end result from the weighted pairwise comparisons by all respondents across all demographic quotas. The comparison matrices for each category are weighted according to the weight vector of the comparisons of the categories.

Table 3) Weighted Priority Vector of the Full Sample n=683 for Choosing the Location of a new Apartment. Source: Own Illustration.

Full Sample		
Rank	**Criterion**	**Relative Weight**
1	Natural amenities	12.07%
2	Shops	11.89%
3	Consumer goods and services	8.10%
4	Public safety	7.98%
5	Connection to public transportation	7.96%
6	Distance to work	7.76%
7	Distance to CBD	6.41%
8	Climate	5.89%
9	Public hygiene	4.54%
10	Environmental protection	4.06%
11	Nightlife	3.99%
12	Cultural offerings	3.78%
13	Architecture/Cityscape	3.59%
14	Connection to long-distance traffic	3.44%
15	Quality of the educational institutions	3.38%
16	Quality of the public administration	2.67%
17	Sports facilities	2.49%

n=683

Table 3 reveals that natural amenities play the most important role among location preferences. Second ranks the availability of shops together with consumer goods and services. Public safety ranks fourth. Sports facilities or the quality of public administration and educational institutions play effectively no role. However, the differences across the 8 least important criteria are minor, which means that they are equally unimportant to the respondents.

Table 4) Weighted Priority Vectors for the Five Generations and the Unweighted Priority Vector for the Categories. Source: Own Illustration.

Category	Silent Generation		Baby Boomer		Generation X		Generation Y		Generation Z	
Aesthetics and physical sourrounding	4	20.81%	3	22.50%	3	22.07%	3	21.11%	4	19.68%
Public services	2	26.46%	4	21.54%	4	21.15%	4	21.00%	2	25.79%
Transportation	3	23.94%	2	25.18%	2	26.31%	2	26.91%	3	25.10%
Localised goods and services	1	28.79%	1	30.78%	1	30.48%	1	30.97%	1	29.42%
Criterion	**Silent Generation**		**Baby Boomer**		**Generation X**		**Generation Y**		**Generation Z**	
Sports facilities	17	1.89%	17	2.00%	16	2.84%	16	3.21%	16	3.59%
Consumer goods and services	5	8.18%	4	8.40%	4	8.13%	4	7.85%	6	6.55%
Shops	2	11.27%	2	13.07%	2	12.03%	1	11.49%	1	9.55%
Nightlife	14	3.29%	11	3.82%	11	3.80%	9	4.69%	9	6.01%
Cultural offerings	10	4.16%	12	3.49%	12	3.67%	13	3.73%	15	3.71%
Architecture/Cityscape	12	3.55%	13	3.32%	10	3.84%	15	3.44%	14	4.18%
Climate	7	5.70%	8	5.57%	8	6.02%	7	6.19%	8	6.01%
Natural amenities	1	11.55%	1	13.61%	1	12.21%	2	11.49%	2	9.49%
Quality of the public administration	13	3.30%	15	2.61%	17	2.30%	17	2.45%	17	2.87%
Environmental protection	9	4.81%	10	4.07%	14	3.52%	14	3.66%	11	5.09%
Public hygiene	8	5.53%	9	4.54%	9	4.22%	11	3.89%	12	4.45%
Public safety	4	9.69%	5	7.93%	5	7.54%	5	6.95%	5	6.98%
Quality of the educational institutions	15	3.14%	16	2.39%	13	3.58%	10	4.06%	7	6.40%
Distance to work	16	3.10%	3	8.44%	3	10.82%	3	10.69%	4	7.20%
Distance to CBD	6	6.46%	7	6.39%	7	6.05%	8	6.02%	10	5.25%
Connection to long-distance traffic	11	3.62%	14	2.73%	15	3.05%	12	3.77%	13	4.43%
Connection to public transportation	3	10.77%	6	7.63%	6	6.38%	6	6.43%	3	8.23%
Number of participants		157		162		180		143		41

Comparison of Generations

The generation comparison of Table 4 provides interesting insights on how the preferences differ among older and younger individuals. The category part at the top of Table 4 shows that localised goods and services play the key role for all generations. Public services are increasingly important to the *Silent Generation* and *Generation Z*, but not for the generations in between. This is not surprising because both groups have the highest exposure to public services; for the *Silent Generation* it is healthcare and for *Generation Z* it is education. For the working generations of the *Baby Boomers*, *X*, and *Y Transportation* is more important than *Public Services*. Surprisingly, *Aesthetics and physical surrounding* play a subordinate role for all generations.

The detailed analysis of the criteria, however, puts natural amenities, such as waterfront or mountains, at the top for the older three generations and second for *Generations X*, *Y*, and *Z*. This reflects the Zeitgeist: nature becomes increasingly important in the eyes of the German population. This can also be observed in the rise of the *Green Party* in recent years and the environment as a dominant political topic. Climate is not of much importance, which is also not surprising given that the climate does not vary much across Germany.

For the *Silent Generation* and *Generation Z* public transportation ranks third, whereas it ranks only 6th for the other three groups. The elderly and the young depend on public transportation to stay mobile. For the former, driving becomes increasingly difficult, and for the latter, driving is out of the question because of the age requirement for a driver's license or the cost of owning a car. The middle generations do not depend on public transportation as much and rank it lower in importance. For them, the distance to work is much more important (3rd rank). This also holds true for *Generation Z*, with the twist that the distance to school also matters. For the *Silent Generation*, distance to work matters little, which is not a surprise as most members of this generation are retired. Long distance-traffic is not a priority criterion for any of the generations. The older the respondents are, the more important is closeness to the CBD, which is plausible in combination with the ranking of Shops on two of the three oldest generations. However, *Generations Y* and *Z* also prefer locations with shopping possibilities as it is the most important criterion.

Although nightlife is generally more important to the younger respondents, it does not play a significant role in choosing a location. For the older respondents cultural offerings are more important relative to the other criteria. Public safety is equally important for all groups and ranks among the top criteria and the most important public service. The criterion *Consumer goods and services* plays an important role for the middle-aged generations; it is less important for *Generation Z* and the *Silent Generation*. Family responsibilities may explain the difference. If children are present, groceries and other services nearby are more important. Elderly and young people only must care for themselves and are less dependent on a supermarket being nearby.

Comparison of Eastern and Western Germany

Table 5) Weighted Priority Vectors for Western German Respondents (left) and Eastern German Respondents (right). Source: Own Illustration.

Western Germany			Eastern Germany		
Rank	**Criterion**	**Relative Weight**	**Rank**	**Criterion**	**Relative Weight**
1	Natural amenities	12.17%	1	Natural amenities	11.61%
2	Shops	12.03%	2	Shops	11.29%
3	Consumer goods and services	8.00%	3	Connection to public transportation	8.92%
4	Distance to work	7.99%	4	Public safety	8.73%
5	Public safety	7.78%	5	Consumer goods and services	8.50%
6	Connection to public transportation	7.72%	6	Distance to work	6.81%
7	Distance to CBD	6.60%	7	Distance to CBD	5.66%
8	Climate	6.13%	8	Climate	5.01%
9	Public hygiene	4.47%	9	Public hygiene	4.76%
10	Environmental protection	4.08%	10	Quality of the educational institutions	4.65%
11	Nightlife	4.01%	11	Environmental protection	3.97%
12	Cultural offerings	3.73%	12	Cultural offerings	3.96%
13	Architecture/Cityscape	3.60%	13	Nightlife	3.88%
14	Connection to long-distance traffic	3.47%	14	Architecture/Cityscape	3.53%
15	Quality of the educational institutions	3.11%	15	Connection to long-distance traffic	3.30%
16	Sports facilities	2.55%	16	Quality of the public administration	3.18%
17	Quality of the public administration	2.54%	17	Sports facilities	2.26%
n=546			n=137		

The differences between Eastern German states and Western states are not large at first sight. The most important criteria for both people are natural amenities and shops. The two least important ones are sports facilities and the quality of the public administration. Consumer goods and distance to work are more important to people in Western Germany. The reasons could be manifold. One reason could be that in Eastern Germany unemployment is higher. Another could be that consumption is not as important as in Western Germany due to lower incomes or due to the lasting cultural impact of the German Democratic Republic. However, the margins of difference are overall very small and the preferences of individuals between Eastern and Western Germany are quite similar.

Comparison of Tenants and Homeowners

Table 6) Weighted Priority Vectors for Respondents who are Tenants (left) and who are Homeowners (right). Source: Own Illustration.

Tenants		
Rank	Criterion	Relative Weight
1	Natural amenities	11.54%
2	Shops	11.53%
3	Public safety	8.47%
4	Consumer goods and services	8.15%
5	Connection to public transportation	8.11%
6	Distance to work	7.38%
7	Distance to CBD	6.39%
8	Climate	5.89%
9	Public hygiene	4.94%
10	Environmental protection	4.31%
11	Nightlife	3.85%
12	Architecture/Cityscape	3.63%
13	Cultural offerings	3.61%
14	Quality of the educational institutions	3.45%
15	Connection to long-distance traffic	3.34%
16	Quality of the public administration	3.04%
17	Sports facilities	2.37%

n=395

Homeowners		
Rank	Criterion	Relative Weight
1	Natural amenities	13.23%
2	Shops	12.29%
3	Distance to work	8.46%
4	Consumer goods and services	8.09%
5	Connection to public transportation	7.50%
6	Public safety	7.09%
7	Distance to CBD	6.36%
8	Climate	6.04%
9	Nightlife	4.22%
10	Cultural offerings	4.14%
11	Public hygiene	3.85%
12	Architecture/Cityscape	3.63%
13	Environmental protection	3.61%
14	Connection to long-distance traffic	3.48%
15	Quality of the educational institutions	3.28%
16	Sports facilities	2.64%
17	Quality of the public administration	2.10%

n=267

Traditionally, the homeownership in Germany is low compared to other OECD countries; it is lower only in Switzerland (Caldera Sánchez & Andrews, 2011). The reasons are manifold but among the most important reasons is the development of house prices in Germany. Empirically, the homeownership rate strongly correlates with housing prices, which results in a higher homeownership rate if prices increase. The anticipation of increasing prices will lead to a stronger investment in residential real estate to participate in the wealth gains. Analysing the differences in location choice preferences of homeowners and tenants helps to understand if people are willing to buy properties in locations that are of interest for renters or if they would look for different locations (Arnold, Rottke, & Winter, 2017, p. 189).

Interestingly, the number of homeowners in the sample is close to the current homeownership rate, although homeownership was not part of a quota. 40% of respondents live in their own house, while 51% of inhabitants are homeowners in the population at large (Eurostat, 2019). For both groups, natural amenities and shops are the most important. Interestingly, for homeowners the distance to work is more relevant than for tenants, which indicates the long-term decision homeowners undertake because they depend on the convenience of being close to work. Public safety is the third most important criterion for tenants. The interpretation is not as straight forward. It could be that tenants are on average less wealthy than homeowners and will have more constraints in choosing a location. In this context it is important to remember that the ranking is conditioned on the respondents' current financial situation. Hence, tenants from less wealthy neighbourhoods, which tend to have higher crime rates, rank this criterion higher in making a choice (Tita et al., 2006). In sum, homeowners put more emphasis on a short distance to employers or business parks, while renters value most public safety.

Comparison by City Size

According to Glaeser et al. (2001), larger cities are more successful economically because people can consume more amenities and will be willing to pay higher rents and higher prices to live there. Germany is a country with a strong federal tradition, which means that economic activity is widely distributed among many cities rather than focused on just a few as in France or England. Berlin "only" has 3.5 million inhabitants, which is comparably small to the Île-de-France (Greater Paris), London, or New York City. The smallest among the largest 20 cities in Germany is Münster, with around 310.000 inhabitants. Internationally, cities are categorized into 4 types (Figure 7): large cities with more than 100.000 inhabitants, medium-sized towns with more than 20.000 but less than 100.000 inhabitants, small towns with more than 5.000 and less than 20.000 inhabitants, and rural communities with less than 5.000 inhabitants (Fuhrich, 2009).

Table 7) Weighted Priority Vectors for Respondents Living in Large Cities (top left), Medium-Sized Towns (top right), Small Towns (bottom left) and Rural Communities (bottom right). Source: Own Illustration.

Large Cities		
Rank	Criterion	Relative Weight
1	Shops	12.18%
2	Natural amenities	10.75%
3	Connection to public transportation	8.93%
4	Consumer goods and services	8.31%
5	Public safety	7.97%
6	Distance to work	6.54%
7	Distance to CBD	6.08%
8	Climate	5.90%
9	Public hygiene	4.85%
10	Nightlife	4.35%
11	Environmental protection	4.26%
12	Architecture/Cityscape	4.24%
13	Cultural offerings	3.94%
14	Quality of the educational institutions	3.24%
15	Connection to long-distance traffic	3.07%
16	Quality of the public administration	2.78%
17	Sports facilities	2.61%

n=234

Medium-Sized Town		
Rank	Criterion	Relative Weight
1	Natural amenities	11.70%
2	Shops	11.20%
3	Consumer goods and services	8.54%
4	Public safety	8.44%
5	Distance to work	7.93%
6	Connection to public transportation	7.31%
7	Distance to CBD	6.97%
8	Climate	6.05%
9	Public hygiene	4.56%
10	Nightlife	3.98%
11	Quality of the educational institutions	3.87%
12	Environmental protection	3.75%
13	Cultural offerings	3.68%
14	Architecture/Cityscape	3.44%
15	Connection to long-distance traffic	3.42%
16	Quality of the public administration	2.77%
17	Sports facilities	2.40%

n=189

Small Town		
Rank	Criterion	Relative Weight
1	Shops	12.48%
2	Natural amenities	12.41%
3	Connection to public transportation	8.35%
4	Public safety	8.14%
5	Distance to work	7.79%
6	Consumer goods and services	7.57%
7	Distance to CBD	6.89%
8	Climate	5.47%
9	Public hygiene	4.42%
10	Environmental protection	4.14%
11	Connection to long-distance traffic	3.97%
12	Cultural offerings	3.94%
13	Nightlife	3.52%
14	Quality of the educational institutions	2.99%
15	Architecture/Cityscape	2.91%
16	Quality of the public administration	2.56%
17	Sports facilities	2.46%

n=144

Rural Communitiy		
Rank	Criterion	Relative Weight
1	Natural amenities	15.12%
2	Shops	11.63%
3	Distance to work	10.02%
4	Consumer goods and services	7.62%
5	Public safety	6.99%
6	Connection to public transportation	6.55%
7	Climate	6.04%
8	Distance to CBD	5.49%
9	Environmental protection	4.06%
10	Public hygiene	4.02%
11	Nightlife	3.85%
12	Connection to long-distance traffic	3.51%
13	Architecture/Cityscape	3.49%
14	Cultural offerings	3.41%
15	Quality of the educational institutions	3.39%
16	Sports facilities	2.42%
17	Quality of the public administration	2.39%

n=116

The top priorities of respondents with respect to location do not appear to differ much between respondents from cities of different sizes according to Figure 10. For all sizes, natural amenities and shops are among the top two priorities. The distance to work becomes more important for smaller towns. Public safety plays a vital role for all town sizes and ranks in the top third. The quality of the public administration and sports facilities are not important for any town size. Yet, the connection to long-distance traffic is important for smaller towns, which could indicate that individuals from smaller towns need to leave their town more often and depend on good train and highway connections. The other criteria do play a similar role for all town sizes. Overall, the differences lie in the transportation amenities, whereas the aesthetical aspects and the localised goods and services are preferred equally across town sizes.

2.5 Discussion

In what follows, our results will be compared with the findings from other empirical studies that used either survey or expert data. Based on our results, all groups consider shopping facilities and natural amenities the two dominant priorities. Bender et al. (1997)used survey data from the Geneva area to evaluate the priorities of single-family home owners. Natural amenities also turn out to be the dominant factor. It is of course difficult to directly compare the results because the criteria differ in number and description. For example, *Quietness* is not included in our list of criteria, which is the second most important one for single-family homeowners in Geneva. Furthermore, schooling is much more important in the Geneva sample than in the German sample. One can only speculate about the reasons as the quality of schooling should not differ much between Switzerland and Germany. One reason could be the phrasing of the criterion; in our questionnaire the term *educational institutions* is used not *schools* as in the Geneva sample. Respondents to the Geneva survey may be thinking about their children's schools, which would explain a higher prioritization.

In general, the existing studies all use different criteria, which makes comparisons more difficult. Also, this study uses a variety of criteria to get an in-depth understanding of the prioritization. Bender et al. (1997) use 8 criteria, Bender et al. (Bender et al., 1999) use 8 criteria but for commercial users. Kauko (2006) employ 6 criteria for residential locations in Helsinki and Randstad, and Kauko (2007) rely on 5 criteria for residential locations in Budapest. Saaty (1986) selects 9 criteria for defining the most liveable city in the US. In essence, the criteria of this paper are a combination of all the above and represent an effort to get a more comprehensive account. For future research, it may be useful to define a standard set of urban amenities as criteria in order to allow for a better comparability among studies.

2.6 Conclusion

The paper analyses the residential location preferences of German residents with the help of the AHP methodology. The AHP methodology makes it possible to model complex decision-making problems by using pairwise comparisons to identify a priority vector of the preferences of the decision makers.

This study relies on a set of survey questions that respondents are supposed to answer conditional on the assumption that they look for the location of an apartment given their current financial constraints. 683 respondents completed the pairwise comparisons of 17 location criteria and provided further information on their socio-economic background.

The analysis generated (a) an overall priority vector of criteria conditioned on treating all respondents as a homogeneous group and (b) a number of priority vectors for different subsamples of the respondents, conditioned on selected socio-demographic variables.

The priority vector for the full sample showed that natural amenities and shopping facilities are the two top criteria by a large margin. This is accordance with previous research that also ranks natural amenities at the top among residential consumers. Transportation amenities, such as the distances to work or to the CBD, also rank among the top priorities. By contrast, recreational facilities and the quality of the public administration play only minor roles. Public safety, which translates into a low crime rate, is important for all demographic cohorts; it ranks between 3rd and 5th place.

On the basis of subsamples of the respondents, some interesting differences in location preferences emerge. For age cohorts, the results agree in general with the expectations one attaches to different age groups. Regardless of the age group, shopping facilities and natural amenities are important for all generations or age groups. Older respondents (the *Silent Generation*) put little value on the distance to work, which is not surprising given that most of them are retirees. Public transportation is important for the young and the old as both depend on public transportation for their mobility. Similarly, Germans from East Germany seem to be more dependent on public transportation as they prefer a good public transportation much more than Western Germans. The margins of the priorities, however, are often quite small and the differences in preferences are sometimes neglectable.

The results for homeowners versus tenants show that homeowners prefer to live close to work, whereas public safety assumes priority for tenants. Respondents from smaller towns prefer to look for apartments that are close to work. Access to public transportation is more important for respondents from larger cities.

Further research should focus on finding sets of criteria that are the same across studies and to establish a standard procedure for conducting research using AHP. Bender et al. (1997) noted that applying the AHP methodology to census-based data has not been tried; yet, this could help to create nationwide location quality indices. Conducting a census-based survey would beyond the scope and abilities of this research paper but the data set obtained during this research would allow to further evaluate the priorities of other geographical units and socio-demographic groups.

3 The Impact of Migration on Real Estate Prices in an Urban Environment[11]

3.1 Introduction

According to the United Nations (UN) the number of international migrants reached a total of 256 million people worldwide in 2017. Germany ranks second behind the United States in terms of percentage of inhabitants of which at least one parent was not born in Germany (UN, 2017). Economists have long been discussing the effect of immigration on real estate markets. Most research has been focused on typical immigration countries such as the United States, Australia, Canada and New Zealand, while empirical research in Germany and other European countries has been scarce. Therefore, this article expands the empirical research by using fixed-effect methodology with the established 'shift-share' - instrumental variable approach to derive the price impact of immigration on housing prices in Berlin. Furthermore, we are extending the academic literature by employing a dynamic difference-in-difference methodology that controls for geographical origin of the immigrant population.

The most prominent immigration study is the one by Card (2001). He used the impact of the Mariel boatlift[12] as a natural experiment on the Miami property and job market. Several other studies looked at the reactions of real estate markets to immigration. Bourassa and Hendershott (Bourassa & Hendershott, 1995) analysed real estate between the years of 1979 and 1993 in the major Australian cities of Brisbane, Canberra and Sydney. They concluded that, apart from its impact on wages and employment, immigration was one of the major drivers of price increases in real estate markets. Similar research was conducted by Ley and Tutchener (2001), who analysed the property markets in the eight largest cities of Canada. The authors concluded that immigration had a strong correlation with increasing house prices. Saiz (2003) notes that economic cycles may play an important role in the analysis of price effects on real estate. He estimates the

11 This chapter is based on a paper written in co-authorship with Heiko Kirchhain.

12 The Mariel boatlift is a large immigration wave from Cubans to the city of Miami where 125.000 Cubans fled the country from the port of Mariel in 1980.

J. de Graaff, *Essays on the Impact of Urban (Dis-)Amenities on the German Real Estate Market*, Essays in Real Estate Research 18,
https://doi.org/10.1007/978-3-658-31623-5_3

elasticity of real estate rental prices with respect to the population to be around unity. He analysed the development of rental prices with respect to immigration in the United States. Due to budget constraints, most immigrants must rent upon arrival (Weiss, 2000). Hence, any impact on the homeownership rate may come with a time delay. Furthermore, a large inflow of immigrants does not in general lead to the same increase in demand as a corresponding increase in the native population. As many immigrants come from poorer countries, the largest effect can be witnessed in low-priced housing segments (Saiz, 2003). On average, the results of the current literature suggest a price elasticity of 0.14 to 1 percent in housing rents (Latif, 2015; Saiz & Saat, 2007).

Furthermore, Stillman and Maré (Stillman & Maré, 2012) conducted research on housing prices in New Zealand. While they did not identify a significant impact of immigration on the real estate prices, they found that returning natives increase prices significantly. Akbary and Aydede (2012) conclude that inflow of immigrants does not negatively influence prices, but that immigrants slow down price growth as it inhibits construction activity in areas with high immigration. In stark contrast, Ley and Tutchener (2001) uncovered a strong correlation between immigration and house prices for Vancouver and Toronto.

More recent research focuses on other countries that are currently major destinations for immigration. Gonzalez and Ortega (2013) look at the causal effect of immigration on Spanish real estate prices during the boom years of the early 2000s. Their approach includes instruments adapting the classical network theory of immigrants by Card (2001) and the gateway theory by e.g. Ley and Tutchener (2001). The authors conclude that the residential markets of Spain were proportionally affected by migration and that immigrants were responsible for a 25 percent increase in housing prices and a 50 percent increase in housing stock. Kalantaryan (2013) examined the price effects of immigration on the real estate prices in Italian provinces. Italy has different characteristics than other industrialized countries as historically more people emigrated than immigrated. The results show that immigration has a positive impact on price appreciation in Italy but with a different distribution across the country. Accetturo et. al. (2014) analysed the prices for different Italian cities on the district level and concludes that immigration increases prices on a city level but on a city quarter level price growth is reduced. Furthermore, they provide evidence of native flight because of negative effects of immigration on perceived local amenities.

There is limited empirical research on German speaking countries. Eilers et al. (2017) use asking price and socio-economic panel data on a zip-code level and show that immigrants do not pay a price premium compared to natives. Most recently Kürschner (2017) uses the natural experiment of the fall of the Berlin Wall estimating an increase of approximately 3.3% due to an 1% increase immigration from East-Germany to West-German urban districts. For Switzerland, Degen & Fischer (2017) use annual data of Swiss statistical areas resembling the MSAs in the United States. They conclude by using the shift-share instrumental variable approach by Card (2001) that natives tend to be crowded out during times of high immigration if immigrants are concentrating in areas due to network effects. These findings are especially relevant for the German market as the Swiss real estate market shows similarities due to its comparable home ownership rate.

In sum, the more recent studies show that the results on the relationship between immigration and housing prices depends on the market, the available data, and the used methodology. From a theoretical point of view, the literature elaborates on two mechanisms that explain whether the house or rental prices are positively or negatively correlated to immigration. Firstly, immigration leads to a demand shift that increases prices in the short term due to an inelastic supply of housing. Secondly, immigration might lead to an outflow of the native population, which will reduce the demand in specific neighbourhoods. Immigrants might be perceived as a disamenity by the native population. This would set the native population worse-off in terms of the consumption of urban amenities, which would lead to a price decrease. The latter case is discussed in most of the recent literature, especially for European markets. Accetturo et. al. (2014), Sá (2015), and Braakmann (Braakmann, 2019) are examples of this branch of the literature. These studies conclude that immigration has a negative impact due to native outmigration.

The contradicting results in the academic literature indicate that, due to major differences of host-country and immigration groups, every country and every immigration wave requires a unique analysis. The study adds several aspects to the current literature: The uniqueness of the dataset allows us to analyse differences of the country of origin of immigrant groups and to compare the effects on apartment and rental prices. Secondly, the analysis is conducted on a neighbourhood level, which allows us to conduct the currently most detailed analysis of the effect of immigration on a specific real estate market in Germany, the capital of Berlin.

Our research is structured as follows: the second section provides an overview of the immigration history of the Federal Republic of Germany and provides detailed information of migration patterns to the city of Berlin; the third section presents our unique dataset; section four explains our methodology in detail; section five documents the empirical results; section six discusses these results against the background of the current academic literature. Section 7 concludes.

3.2 Immigration to Germany and Berlin since 1950

3.2.1 Immigration History of the Federal Republic of Germany

Since the end of the World War II, Germany[13] experienced several immigration waves. In 2017, 17.1 million people with migration background were living in Germany, which accounts for 21 percent of the total population.[14] Figure 1 illustrates the total net migration balance for Germany since the year 1950.

During the 1950s the German economy grew rapidly resulting in a workforce shortage. Therefore, Germany negotiated contracts with several countries from Eastern and Southern Europe in order to allow workers from those countries to immigrate to Germany for work. The first contract was negotiated between Germany and Italy (1955), followed by contracts with Spain (1960) Greece and Turkey (1961), Morocco (1963), Tunisia (1965), and Yugoslavia (1968). At the beginning, the number of what was referred to as "guest workers" was relatively small (330,000).

---

13 Germany was divided until 1990. In this context we are assuming a single state body.

14 Migration Background is defined as: "all persons who have immigrated into the territory of today's Federal Republic of Germany after 1949, and of all foreigners born in Germany and all persons born in Germany who have at least one parent who immigrated into the country or was born as a foreigner in Germany." (Statistisches Bundesamt, 2019)

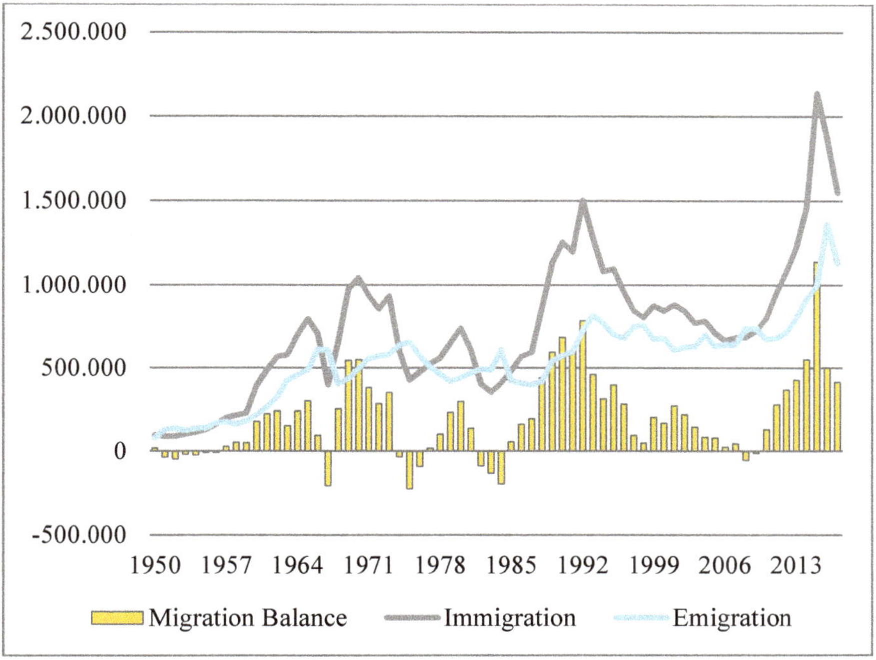

Figure 6) Immigration, Emigration and Migration Balance of Germany From 1950 Until 2015[15], Source: Statistisches Bundesamt (2017).

But the numbers rapidly increased after the building of the Berlin Wall in 1963 because the internal migration flow between the two German states stopped abruptly. The guest worker programs were effectively terminated as a consequence of a period of slow economic growth during the oil crisis in the 1970s. In 1973, 4 million migrants already lived in Germany (Münz & Ulrich, 2000). Originally, these programs were designed to allow for work migration but many immigrants, mainly men, found a new home in Germany and never left. This led to a further increase in migration because the German government allowed their families to immigrate to Germany as well.

15 Until 1990 West-Germany, from 1950 until 1957 without the Federal-State "Saarland".

The next immigration wave arrived from late-resettled-families.[16] This group consisted in large part of German minorities from Eastern European countries, mostly from today's Ukraine and Kazakhstan (formerly parts of the Soviet Union), Poland, and Romania, who returned to the country of their ancestors. In treaties with Eastern Europe between 1970 and 1973 between West-Germany and the relevant states, German minorities were granted the right of free movement and to return to Germany. By the 1980s, 1.5 million of these migrants had entered Germany. An additional 2.5 million people used the same channel between 1988 and 1998 after the fall of the Berlin Wall.

Following the civil war in the former state of Yugoslavia, another large immigration wave took place that included mostly asylum seekers from Balkan states (Brücker, Hauptmann, & Vallizadeh, 2015). In 1992, the immigration peaked with 438,000 people applying for political asylum in Germany. The net migration amounted to approximately 700,000 people in this year, including asylum seekers from Yugoslavia and other immigrants from the former Soviet republics. During the turbulent years after the fall of the Berlin Wall, 1.5 million people immigrated to Germany as a result of being granted political asylum. Many of these would later bring 2.5 million family members to Germany.

Between 1995 and 2015, immigrants came mainly from EU-member states but with lower numbers of net immigration. Between 1995 and 2005, the German economy struggled with high unemployment and low economic growth, which made Germany unattractive for work migration. Consequently, in- and outmigration was balanced. The numbers started to increase again after the admission of the 13 Eastern European states to the European Union after 2004. Furthermore, economic and fiscal crises in the aftermath of the global financial crisis in Southern Europe lead to an increase in net-migration to Germany for economic reasons. Between 1995 and 2015, 13.9 million people immigrated to Germany, while 11.1 million left the country, which amounts to a net-migration of 2.8 million people in 20 years or 233.000 per year.

---

16 German: „Spätaussiedler“,

The most recent large immigration wave is commonly known to as the "refugee crisis". This term refers to a major immigration wave to Europe caused by the turmoil in the Middle Eastern countries in the aftermath of the Arab Spring and the ongoing civil wars in Syria, Afghanistan and Iraq. In total, 3.1 million people emigrated between 2014 and 2016 from mostly Muslim countries to the European Union, with the main destinations being Austria, Germany, Hungary and Sweden (Eurostat, 2018). Germany registered, in the year 2015 alone, a total of 722,370 people seeking asylum (BAMF, 2018). Including non-refugee immigration, 2.14 million people immigrated to Germany, while 1 million left the country, which generated a surplus of 1.15 million people just in 2015. For comparison, the second biggest net-immigrant country in the EU is the United Kingdom (UK), with a net migration of 400.000 people (Eurostat, 2018). The year 2015 saw by far the largest annual immigration wave in the history of post-war Germany. The large number of immigrants overwhelmed the public institutions, the housing market and caused major shifts in the German political landscape. In total, 1.6 million people migrated to Germany since 2014 seeking asylum, with most people arriving from Syria (454.000), Afghanistan (191.000) and Iraq (156.500) (Statistisches Bundesamt, 2017).

3.2.2 *Submarket Berlin*

Due to its unique history, Berlin represents a special case regarding immigration policies. Until 1990, the German capital was divided as the aftermath of the Second World War. While West-Berlin experienced similar immigration waves as the rest of West-Germany, East-Germany did not. Figure 7 shows the percentage of the population of the individual city quarters with a migration background. Evidently, Berlin was not only divided by the Berlin-Wall but remains divided regarding the number of people with a migration background. Berlin absorbed approx. 60.000 asylum seekers during 2015 and 2016, which is a little less than 2% of the total population (BAMF, 2016). However, Berlin also experienced a net migration from other parts of Europe and from Germany due to various reasons, which assumingly puts pressure on the housing market. Furthermore, the public governance of the inflow of immigrants was comparably chaotic (Müchler, 2015).

At the end of 2017, 3.712 million people were living in Berlin, with 1.2 million of those with migration background, which accounts for 32% of the total population. The breakdown of the migrant population by geographical origin is as follows: from other EU-countries (386.000), Turkey (180.000), Arab states (140.000), former Yugoslavia (62.000), the former Soviet Union (123.000), others (250.000), not identifiable (68.000). Given the size of the market, the relatively isolated geographic position, as well as pronounced price and demographic variations, Berlin can be considered a perfect candidate for the analysis of price patterns due to immigration in Germany.

3.3 Data

Our dataset for analysing the impact of migration on residential real estate prices was constructed from various commercial and public sources. It is combined to a partially unbalanced panel data set with n=447 cross section units observed over t=6 time periods. The data for the Berlin residential real estate market is provided by a commercial appraisal firm from Germany and contains the residential rents (*rent*) and the sales prices of apartments in multi-family homes (*etw*). The prices and rents are collected by the data provider and are aggregated to the statistical level of so called "life-oriented spaces" (LOR). Overall, the data is available annually for 447 LORs from 2012 to 2017.

The LORs are statistical units that include relatively homogeneous and comparable demographics. The primary goal is to focus the borders of the statistical units more on the social structure of the area rather than on its geographical organization. The reasoning by the authorities is that statistical blocks usually follow solely large transportation routes and streets but omit socio-economic context.

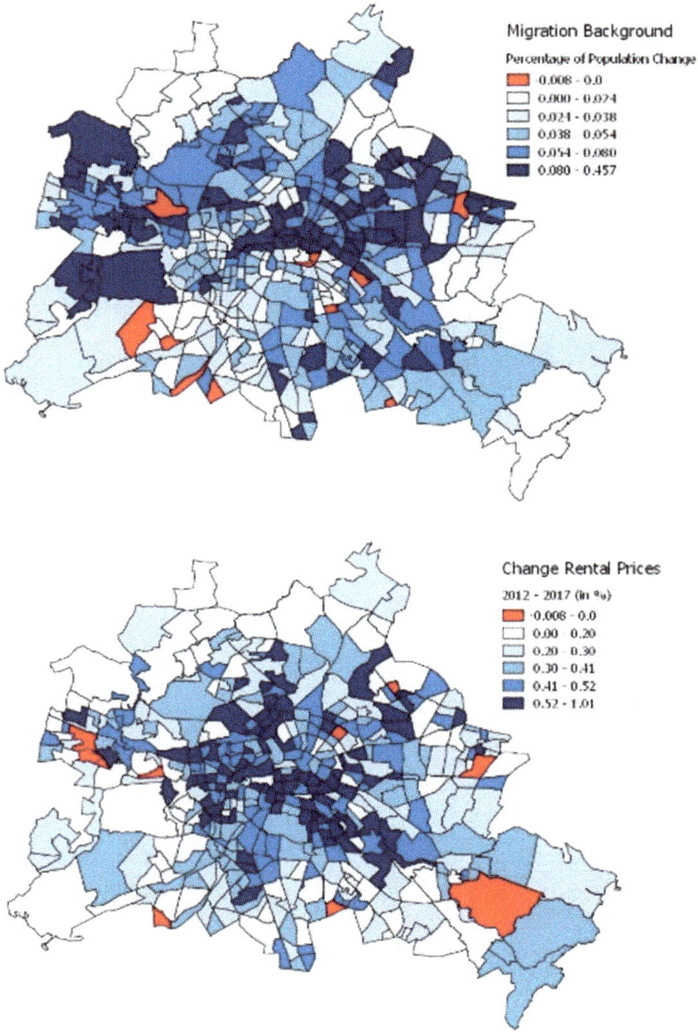

Figure 7) Spatial Distribution Change of Migration (top), Change in Rental Prices (bottom). Source: Own Illustration.

Table 8) Summary Statistics. Source: Own Illustration.

Variable	Obs	Mean	Std. Dev.	Min	Max	Description
Residential rents	1,588	9.17	1.95	4.22	16.88	Average rent per square meter in €
Apartment prices	1,415	2,977.90	1,202.38	758.80	9,589.85	Average sales prices per square meter in €
Inhabitants	1,602	8,897.46	5,582.41	9.00	35,951.00	Number of inhabitants
German	1,602	6,222.17	4,248.03	0.00	31,079.00	Number of inhabitants of German origin
Migrants	1,602	2,675.29	2,451.30	6.00	16,654.00	Number of total migrants
EU-28	1,602	914.50	794.79	0.00	4,972.00	Number of migrants from the EU-28 states
EU-15	1,604	445.03	500.32	0.00	3,481.00	Number of migrants from the EU-15 states
EU-13	1,602	468.92	406.37	0.00	3,221.00	Number of migrants from the EU-13 states
Arab	1,604	243.35	323.09	0.00	2,409.00	Number of migrants from Arab states
Turkish	1,604	414.60	750.78	0.00	5,857.00	Number of migrants from Turky
Polish	1,604	249.54	211.19	0.00	1,354.00	Number of migrants from Poland
Former Yugoslavia	1,604	147.31	183.98	0.00	1,596.00	Number of migrants from former Yugoslavia
Former Sovjet Unioı	1,604	240.09	200.45	0.00	1,693.00	Number of migrants from the former Sovjet Union
Unknown	1,602	167.01	197.97	0.00	1,443.00	Number of migrants where origin is unknown
Others	1,602	547.56	453.47	0.00	2,482.00	Number of migrants from other nationalities
Population density	1,602	9,570.45	7,250.25	10.03	33,453.08	Number of inhabitants per square kilometer
Welfare recipients	1,457	0.25	0.15	0.00	0.98	Number of welfare recipients
Migration quota	1,602	0.30	0.16	0.02	1.00	Share of inhabitants with a migration background of total inhabitant

The rents are collected as the average rental price per square meter in Euro for each LOR. The apartment prices are denoted as absolute prices per square meter sold space in Euro. Due to some missing data points, the data set contains 1,588 observations for the rents and 1,415 data points for the apartment prices. Summary statistics and a short description of the data are provided in Table 3. The control variables are obtained from the statistical office of the state of Berlin as well as the administrative office for integration, employment and social welfare of Berlin. The data contain various socio-demographic variables as well as information about the ethnic background of the people living in the respective LOR.

The data set contains information about the following citizenships and ethnicities that are permanent residents in Berlin and represent the largest groups of immigrants: European Union *(eu)*, Turkish *(turk)*, Arab *(arab)*, Polish *(polen)*, former Soviet Union *(ehesu)*, former Yugoslavia *(ehejug)*, unknow origin *(nzord)* and other nationalities *(sonst)*. Furthermore, the dataset contains the total amount of inhabitants with a migration background (*mh*) and differentiates between the EU-15[17] states and the EU-28. The number of immigrants from the 13 states that entered the European Union after 2004 were derived by subtracting the EU-15 states from the EU-28 and are named EU-13[18]. We calculate this figure because we expect a different socio-economic background Overall, we assume that migrants from those countries are on average poorer and less well educated than migrants from the EU-15 states.

Additional to the migrant variables, we include several socio-demographic control variables provided by the statistical office of Berlin. Firstly, we use the share of immigrants in the respective LOR to control for the a priori level of all immigrants. The reasoning is that there is a difference in perception if the immigrant population increases in areas where many immigrants already live. Hence, we

17 The 15 founding nations of the EU in 2004 were: Belgium, Denmark, Germany, Finland, France, Greece, Ireland, Italy, Luxemburg, Netherlands, Austria, Portugal, Sweden, Spain, and the United Kingdom.

18 The 13 states that entered the EU between 2004 and 2013 in the order of accession: Estonia, Latvia, Lithuania, Malta, Poland, Slovakia, Slovenia, Cech Republic, Hungary, Cyprus, Bulgaria, Romania, Croatia.

expect that a percentage increase in an area with a low initial foreign share will have a stronger impact than in an area with initially higher shares. Furthermore, we control for population density (*pop_density*), which is the number of inhabitants per square kilometre, to account for the level of urbanity of each LOR (Glaeser et al., 2001, p. 46). Unfortunately, the dataset does not contain any information about income or education of the inhabitants, which is why we use the number of people receiving social welfare *(sozh)* as an approximation. The idea is that the higher the number of people receiving social welfare the lower the average income of the people as we expect a segregation regarding income between neighbourhoods. As shown in Appendix B, the price data are not normally distributed, which is why all prices are transformed by taking the natural logarithm. The same holds true for population density.

3.4 Methodology

The empirical strategy is twofold. In the first part we will follow the approach by Acceturo et al. (2014) and apply a standard panel data methodology using fixed-effects. We also include an instrumental variable approach by Card (2001) to account for endogeneity and allow for casual inference. We will also account for recent criticism of the chosen instrumental variable approach by Jaeger, Ruist and Stuhler (2017), who recommend to break down the total migration data into ethnicities. As our dataset contains information on the largest ethnicities that migrated to Berlin, we will be able to follow this recommendation in our analysis.

The second part will analyse potential non-linear reactions of real estate submarkets depending on assumed different absorption reactions of the individual neighbourhoods depending on demographic composition. Therefore, we are employing a difference-in-difference approach using a treatment variable capturing short-term population shifts by ethnicity in each LOR. Henceforth, we will analyse part I and part II separately and compare the results in the discussion.

3.4.1 Part I: Panel with Fixed-Effects and IV Approach

Part I focuses on the relationship between the number of all migrants and the residential rents and apartment prices. The models are estimated separately using the rents and the prices as dependent variables. Since prices and rents are not normally distributed, the natural logarithm is taken for both measures.

The empirical model is estimated using standard fixed-effect methodology with heteroscedastic robust standard errors in the form of:

$$\ln(y_{it}) = \beta_1 m_{e_{it}} + \dots + \beta_k c_{k_{it}} + d_t + a_i + u_{it} \tag{7}$$

where subscript i identifies the LORs (i = 1,…,447) and subscript t the years (t = 1,…,6) years, m_e is the respective number of migrants, c_k is a set of control variables and d_t are time fixed effects; a_i captures all the time-invariant characteristics of the LORs and u_{it} is the error term. The fixed-effects model allows us to control for all time invariant properties of the LOR, which is why we do not have to control for any idiosyncratic properties of the LOR, such as location or urban amenities and disamenities, assuming they do not change in the relatively short time frame of the 6 years of the panel. Yet, the presence of a strong time trend in prices as well as in rents during the observation period from 2012 to 2017 necessitates to include dummy variables for time.[19] The Hausman-test[20] confirms the fixed-effects estimation as appropriate relative to random effects. Since we have a short panel with a relatively large number of participants, we do not expect cross-sectional dependence (Baltagi, 2005, p. 247).

Shift-Share-Instrument

In order to control for reverse causality and omitted variable bias, we are using the shift-share or past settlement instrument. This is a two-stage-least square methodology that has been used in the immigration literature in recent decades.[21] Developed by Card (2001), the idea of this instrument is to exploit the network effects of previously immigrated migrant groups from the same country of origin as the current migrants to a certain region in an individual country. This instru-

---

19 The Wald-test rejects the null-hypothesis that the coefficients for all years are equal to zero. Therefore, time-dummies are incorporated.

20 The Hausman-test is a standard measure to identify whether the fixed-effects or random-effects estimator is appropriate. For further details see Woolridge (2002).

21 See Jaeger et al. (2017) for an overview of current literature.

ment is based on the assumption that immigrant groups seek proximity to their peers from their country-of-origin that already reside in the country they emigrate to. (see, among others, Bartel (1989) and LaLonde and Topel (1991)).[22] The rather intuitive instrument is constructed as follows:

$$S_{LOR,t} = \sum_{i} \pi_{i,LOR,t_0} M_{i,t} \quad (8)$$

The estimated settlement of migrants S at time t to a LOR in Berlin is derived from the initial share of migrant population (π) at time t_0 (in this case the year 2001) multiplied with the current national migration (M) from country i at time t.

For this instrument to work properly, two assumptions must be fulfilled: Firstly, the current stock of migrants does not affect the housing price trend in the individual quarters; secondly, the omitted variables on the district level do not influence the overall immigration on the national level. This can be assumed as the population of each single LOR is too small to influence the total immigration trends to Germany.[23] The main idea of this instrument is that the location decision of the initial immigrant groups is separated from the local housing trends that may affect the location decisions of migrants in the future. The more time lies between the settlement of the previous migrants and the observed influx, the more plausible this separation becomes. In our case, we are using the first year the migrant population was registered on the LOR level, which was the year 2001. This widely employed instrument, however, has received increasing criticism. The exclusion assumption is probably violated due to long term effects of the first immigration wave on the individual city district. This is the case if the initial composition of immigrant groups is not changing. Most recently, Jaeger et

22 The authors additionally argue, that in a high demand market like Berlin it is difficult for certain immigrant groups to find affordable living space in certain areas. Therefore, and because of risk assessment of landlords, long term effects of previous immigrant groups from the same country-of-origin are an in-crowding into migrant areas.

23 In the basis year of the instrument the largest share of migrants from a specific country in comparison to the total number of this immigrant group is in Rixdorf, Neukölln. Here the Arab population accounts for 0.6% of the overall Arab population in Germany. It can therefore be assumed that the price trend in this specific neighborhood does not influence the overall immigration trend from Arab countries to Germany. This holds especially true, as we are using time and district fixed-effects panel data.

al. (2018) are concluding in a working paper that a large disruption of the country-of-origin composition of the migrants must occur in order to identify valid short-term causal effects. In our case, during the refugee crisis, this is the case as a large influx of new refugees, mostly from Arab countries, are disrupting the established population composition.[24] While most studies only look at immigrant groups in total, we have the opportunity to control for this fact, which is done in models V and VI.

3.4.2 Part II: Panel with Difference-in-Difference Approach

The analysis of Part I is conducted under the assumption that migration has a log-linear influence on prices. However, one could argue that migration also has a continuous impact on housing prices. There are several reasons why this might be the case. Firstly, the low elasticity of housing supply in the short-term would cause an increase in prices if migrants cause an overall increase of demand in a certain area (Ottaviano & Peri, 2006; Saiz, 2003; Saiz & Saat, 2007). In case of the refugee crisis in Germany, for example, 1.5 million people had to be integrated into the housing market within several months. In case of Berlin, which already had a relatively low vacancy rate during the crisis compared to rural areas in eastern Germany, this would presumably cause an increase in rental and land prices. Secondly, a strong influx of migrants in a relatively short period of time could cause other inhabitants to leave the area and move away because the socio-economic and socio-cultural environment changes in a way that urban amenities are shared by more people, which causes existing inhabitants to suffer a loss in urban amenity consumption. In this case, immigration works as a dis-amenity to natives, which is widely discussed in the racial segregation literature (Saiz & Wachter, 2011, p. 173). However, the decision to move away and decrease the demand under the assumption of an inelastic supply should depend on two things: time and the tolerance of being worse-off. This means, on the one hand, that this is usually a decision not taken easily, which accounts for the fac-

24 Number of Arab migrants increased from approx. 300,000 in 2012 to approx. 1,400,000 in 2017 in Germany. While in 2012 only 7.5% of new arrivals were from Arab countries, this number increased to approx. 90% in 2016

tor time and, on the other hand, that people might tolerate a certain amount of migration for various reasons, but will move if a certain point is exceeded. Hence, an effect might be observed after a certain threshold of increase or decrease of people with a migration background is reached (Card, Mas, & Rothstein, 2008; Schelling, 1978). In the second part of the analysis we, therefore, adapt a difference-in-difference approach by Card, Mas & Rothstein (2008), where a certain change in migration will be the treatment of each LOR to account for the notion that a change in migration might cause a change in prices after a certain threshold is passed.

Methodologically, a treatment dummy is calculated for each observation if a certain threshold of the percentage change of a respective ethnicity is reached in a particular LOR. The treatment dummy depends on the size of the change from one period to the next period. This threshold variable is calculated as the interaction term between the percentage change of the respective migration group and the thresholds stated above:

$d_{thres_{it}} = 1\ if\ \Delta ethnicity_{it} > threshold$, with

$$\Delta ethnicity_{it} = \frac{ethnicity_t}{ethnicity_{t-1}} - 1 \tag{9}$$

Therefore, for every observation that exceeds the threshold in a year, the treatment dummy will be 1 or else 0. For example, in the case of a LOR with 100 Turkish migrants in 2012 and 106 in 2013, the increase would be 6%. The treatment variable would be 1 for thresholds greater than 0%, greater than +1% and greater than +5%, but 0 for all thresholds greater than +10.

Treatment variables are calculated for several thresholds representing the change in the respective ethnicity. The change of each individual ethnicity that is available in our dataset is calculated and regressed on the rental prices as well as the apartment prices (y) with a standard panel data fixed-effects methodology in the form of:

$$y_{it} = \beta_{thres} d_{thres_{it}} + \cdots + \beta_k c_{k_{it}} + d_t + a_i + u_{it} \tag{10}$$

where i = 1…447 LORs and t = 1…6 years d is the respective treatment variable depending on the threshold, and c_k is a set of control variables and d_t are time-dummies. a_i represents each LOR individual time-invariant characteristics and

u_{it} is the error term. The properties of equation (10) are the same as the properties of equation (7); only the treatment dummy is included instead of the number of migrants.

The expectation is that significant effects on prices emerge only after an unknown threshold of change in migrants is passed. This would indicate that not every change in the migrant population has the same impact on prices. It may also be true that the tolerance level of natives is set at different levels for each group of migrants and for migrants overall. We further expect that higher thresholds will yield higher effects because all observations included in lower thresholds are also included in the thresholds above. Yet, the significances for the larger thresholds might be lower due to the smaller number of observations. Furthermore, we assume that a significant result allows us to infer a causal relationship between the change in migrants and the price change because a time-lag is included in the treatment dummy.

3.5 Results

The fixed-effects regressions of models I and III in Table 9 show a negative relationship between rental and apartment prices and the total number of migrants. It is significant at the 1% level. The coefficient of -0.195 means that, for a 10% increase in the number of migrants, rental prices drop be about 2%. For the apartment prices the elasticity of price with respect to the number of migrants is higher at -0.236.[25] Models II and IV (Table 9) indicate a likely bias toward zero for the results from Model I and III. The results, including those based on the shift-share instrument, show an elasticity of migration of - 0.439 for rental prices and of - 0.789 for apartment prices, with both being also significant at the 1% level. The Kleibergen-Paap first stage F-statistics of the instruments exceed the threshold of 10 rejecting the null hypothesis of weak instruments. The models explain between 74% and 79% of the variance in the prices, which is acceptable due to the limited data availability.

---

25 The coefficients represent elasticities as both the dependent and the independent variable are logarithmic measures. The interpretation is, therefore, as the following: $\%\Delta y=\beta 1\%\Delta x$

The fixed-effects estimations show a more differentiated picture if the migration variable is split into the respective ethnicities. Models V and VI in Table 10 show that the Arab ethnic background is the only one with a negative elasticity that is statistically significant. A 10% increase of Arab migrants relates to a quarter percent decrease in rental prices and a half a percent decrease in apartment prices. Turkish, Polish, EU-13, migrants from former Yugoslavia and from other nations do not show significant relationships with our two price measures. EU-15 migrants have a positive impact on rental prices: they increase by 0.35% for a 10% increase of this group. Migrants from the former Soviet Union affect apartment prices negatively by -0.94% for a 10% increase. Inhabitants from unknown origin also have a significant positive relationship to rental prices (0.22%) and apartment prices (0.36%) for a 10% increase. The estimates in Table 10 do not use the instrumental variable approach because the breaking down of the ethnicities is one major improvement to the shift-share instrumental variable approach by Card (2001) that Jaeger, Ruist and Stuhler (2017) proposed in their latest critique.

The results indicate a complicated relationship of demand changes and perceived amenities that ultimately cause prices to increase or decline. The overall negative price effects of immigration are in accordance with the results of Accetturo et. al (2014), Braakman (Braakmann, 2019) and Sá (2015). Their explanation that a negative effect is due to a different valuation of urban amenities by the native population seems also plausible in our case. Table 9 supports their argument, as it shows that a short-term increase in migrants relates to an outflow of native inhabitants. Model VIII in Table 11 shows a significant negative relationship between the number of migrants and the number of Germans. Hence, there is a native outflow in the case of a migration inflow.

However, in contrast to the other studies, we can control for different impacts depending on the ethnicity of the immigrants. While Arab migrants tend to have a negative impact on both apartment and rental prices, EU-migration has a positive impact on rental prices. It is possible that, due to the cultural proximity of EU-migrants, the additional pressure of EU-migrants might be considered as increased demand, therefore causing increased rental prices.[26] By contrast, the additional demand of Arabs may be counterbalanced by a perceived increase of disamenities by the local population, which causes a drop in both rental and apartment prices. The significant positive effect of migrants from unknown origin is unclear.

Table 9) Fixed-Effect Regression with and Without Instrumental Variable of Rental and Apartment Prices on Number of Migrants. Source: Own Illustration.

Dependent Variable	Log of rental prices		Log of apartment prices	
	Model I	Model II	Model III	Model IV
Log of migrants	-0.195 ***	-0.439 ***	-0.236 ***	-0.789 ***
	(-4.73)	*(-2.73)*	*(-2.95)*	*(-2.96)*
Log of population density	0.360 **	0.590 ***	-0.350 *	0.263
	(2.42)	*(3.04)*	*(-1.68)*	*(0.75)*
Welfare recipients	0.005	0.029	-0.026	0.022
	(0.11)	*(0.66)*	*(-0.35)*	*(0.30)*
Share of migrants	0.793 **	1.826 **	1.359	3.468 ***
	(2.49)	*(2.51)*	*(2.38)*	*(3.20)*
Time dummies	Yes	Yes	Yes	Yes
Number of observations	1,456	1,414	1,338	1,315
R^2	0.744	0.734	0.791	0.775
AIC	-4107.7	-3891.4	-2535.1	-2372.3
First Stage:				
Instrument	-	0.000 ***	-	0.000 ***
		(-6.11)		*(-5.92)*
Set of controls included	-	Yes	-	Yes
Time dummies included	-	Yes	-	Yes
F-Statistic on the excluded instrum	-	37.34	-	35.06

Notes: *** p<0.01; ** p<0.05; * p<0.1; Fixed-effect panel regression with robust standard errors.

26 As immigrants usually rent due to budget constraints Weiss (2000),

Table 10) Fixed-Effect Regression of Rental and Apartment Prices on the Number of Migrants of Different Ethnicity. Source: Own Illustration.

Dependent Variable	Log of rental prices	Log of apartment prices
	Model V	Model VI
Log of Arab migrants	-0.025 ***	-0.052 ***
	(-2.92)	(-3.14)
Log of Turkish migrants	-0.010	0.000
	(-0.66)	(-0.01)
Log of Polish migrants	-0.032	-0.062
	(-1.03)	(-1.54)
Log of EU-13 migrants	0.001	0.025
	(0.04)	(0.68)
Log of EU-15 migrants	0.035 **	-0.006
	(2.14)	(-0.12)
Log of former Soviet Union migrar	0.004	-0.094 **
	(0.20)	(-2.50)
Log of former Yugoslavia migrants	-0.013	0.009
	(-1.28)	(0.58)
Log of unknown origin	0.022 ***	0.036 **
	(2.88)	(2.49)
Log of other nationalities	-0.035	0.055
	(-1.55)	(1.06)
Population density	0.275 *	-0.500 **
	(1.86)	(-2.40)
Welfare recipients	-0.018	-0.059
	(-0.41)	(-0.78)
Share of migrants	0.261	0.793
	(0.83)	(1.48)
Time-dummies	Yes	Yes
Number of observations	1438	1331
R^2	0.752	0.798
AIC	-4081.7	-2547.3

Notes: *** p<0.01; ** p<0.05; * p<0.1; Fixed-effect panel regression with robust standard errors.

Table 11) Fixed-Effect Regression of Native Population on the Number of Migrants with and without Instrumental Variable. Source: Own Illustration.

Dependent Variable	Native population	
	Model VII	Model VIII
Log of migrants	-0.040	-0.352 ***
	(-0.68)	*(-7.98)*
Log of population density	5,372 ***	6,227 ***
	12.87	*18.66*
Welfare recipients	87.26 *	44.22
	1.80	*1.05*
Share of migrants	-6,965 ***	-4,286 ***
	(-10.98)	*(-7.98)*
Time dummies	Yes	Yes
Number of observations	1,457	1,414
R^2	0.64	0.47
AIC	16,418	16,522
First Stage:		
Instrument	-	0.99712 ***
Set of controls included	-	Yes
Time dummies included	-	Yes
F-Statistic on the excluded instrum	-	42.09

Notes: *** p<0.01; ** p<0.05; * p<0.1; Fixed-effect panel regression with robust standard errors.

3.5.1 Results Part II:

Rents

The estimations in part II use separate regressions for each threshold and ethnicity. Hence, for each coefficient one regression was run. The results for rental prices show a decrease between 1.0 % and 2.1% for an increase in migrants above 0%, 1%, 5% and above 15% (see Table 12).[27] For robustness reasons, we ran the equations for thresholds from 0% to 10% in steps of 1%. We found negative and statistically significant effects for thresholds of 2%, 3%, 5%, and 8%. All of them were within or slightly below the 1% to 1.5% effect shown in the results.

Overall, a significant negative effect can be observed for an increase of the Arab population during the previous year. Significant results are obtained for all treatment thresholds except for the >5% threshold. Furthermore, the coefficients increase almost throughout all models except for the above 30% and 40% thresholds, which aligns with our expectation that the results for higher thresholds should show a larger effect than those for the lower thresholds. The size of the effect varies between 0.7% and 1.4% depending on the size of the increase. The variable that represents the initial share of migrants is not significant, which indicates that Arabs do not show any systematic clustering across LORs.

An increase in Turkish migrants shows a different relationship as it indicates a positive effect on rental prices. All models show significant results, except for those that relate to the >5% and >10% thresholds. The effect lies between 0.9% and 1.1%; this means that an increase of Turkish migrants of more than 15% increases prices by 1.1% the following year. As Saiz and Wachter (2011, p.173) have pointed out, a negative correlation of the migrant density and prices is a strong sign of segregation and, therefore, enclave building. In our case the density is measured by the share of migrants in an LOR, which allows to take the concentration of one migrant group into account It is highly negatively correlated with rental prices, which indicates a segregation of Turkish migrants from other inhabitants. Hence, the influence of a demand shift of Turkish migrants could cause the prices to increase because of the demand shift and the relatively inelastic supply.

Overall, the increase in EU migrants seems to have a negative effect on rental prices. For both the EU-13 and EU-15 migrants, there are significant negative

27 The interpretation of the coefficients follows the calculation of ebthresdthres, which can be shown easily when taking e to the power of both sides of equation 4 to remove the logarithm. The ratio of LORs with d=1 and d=0 will result in ebthresdthres., with dthres = 1.

effects for several thresholds. For the EU-15 migrants, the significant negative results appear for the thresholds from >0% to >20%; for the EU-13 migrants, statistically significant negative effects only begin to show above the 5% threshold. None of the results for this group of migrants is significant for the thresholds above 20%. This is not easy to explain with a smaller sample size for the >25%, >30% and >40% threshold categories. For example, there are 650 observations in category that relates to an increase of above 25% for the EU-13 migrants.

The interpretation regarding the share is more difficult in the case of the EU-migrants and shows some limitations of the interpretation regarding the enclave building of Turkish migrants. The shares for EU-13 and EU-15 are highly correlated with the rents, which would indicate a clustering of the EU migrants. However, an increase of migrants would then be expected to lead to an increase in prices; but that is not the case. Saiz and Wachter (2011, p. 173) point out in this context that a positive correlation as opposed to a negative correlation does not allow a clear interpretation regarding the presence of enclaves. One interpretation could be that, on average, migrants from both groups live in more expensive neighbourhoods, but tend to decrease the rental prices for an unknown reason. Therefore, when they move out, prices increase. This could be explained either by a demand shock or with the help of the theory of the consumption of urban amenities described in section 1. Natives could be better off if certain people leave that consume a lot of urban amenities. Based on this interpretation, our results would be an indication that EU-migrants consume a lot of urban amenities. However, inference on this subject is extremely difficult because we do not have any information about the socio-economic properties of the different groups. Nevertheless, the effects vary between -0.9% and -1.3% for the EU-13 migrants for all thresholds larger and equal to the >5% threshold, and between -1.3% and -2.1% for migrants from EU-15 countries.

Table 12) Results for the Difference-in-Difference Fixed-Effects Estimation of Rental Prices on Positive Treatments. Source: Own Illustration.

	Dependent Variable: Logs of Rental Prices								
Change in %	>0	>0.01	>0.05	>0.1	>0.15	>0.2	>0.25	>0.3	>0.4
All migrants	-0.021 ***	-0.017 ***	-0.010 **	-0.008	-0.013 *	-0.009	-0.005	-0.015	-0.007
share	-0.189	-0.189	-0.190	-0.204	-0.183	-0.189	-0.205	-0.189	-0.208
Arabs	-0.007 *	-0.007 *	-0.005	-0.007 **	-0.010 ***	-0.011 ***	-0.014 ***	-0.010 **	-0.009 **
share	-0.312	-0.304	-0.326	-0.295	-0.285	-0.274	-0.252	-0.283	-0.304
Turkish	0.009 ***	0.009 ***	0.005	0.004	0.011 **	0.009 *	0.011 *	0.011 *	0.012 *
share	-4.148 ***	-4.140 ***	-4.048 ***	-4.028 ***	-4.078 ***	-4.032 ***	-4.027 ***	-4.011 ***	-3.999 ***
Polish	-0.003	-0.003	0.002	-0.004	-0.004	0.001	0.005	0.009	-0.007
share	-1.785 **	-1.807 **	-2.046 **	-1.823 **	-1.868 **	-1.981 **	-2.043 **	-2.045 **	-1.927 **
EU-13	-0.006	-0.006	-0.009 **	-0.012 ***	-0.012 ***	-0.013 ***	-0.009	-0.008	-0.006
share	0.779 *	0.776 *	0.845 **	0.862 **	0.812 **	0.792 **	0.717 *	0.694 *	0.671 *
EU-15	-0.013 ***	-0.015 ***	-0.021 ***	-0.020 ***	-0.012 ***	-0.010 **	-0.003	0.001	-0.001
share	3.913 ***	3.994 ***	4.098 ***	3.922 ***	3.677 ***	3.628 ***	3.548 ***	3.510 ***	3.528 ***
Soviet Union	0.000	0.001	-0.005	0.001	-0.006	-0.002	0.003	0.005	0.009
share	0.476	0.431	0.704	0.403	0.641	0.497	0.413	0.384	0.374
Yugoslavia	0.004	0.003	0.000	-0.002	-0.001	-0.002	-0.001	-0.003	0.007
share	-3.005 ***	-2.987 ***	-2.845 ***	-2.784 ***	-2.806 ***	-2.799 ***	-2.819 ***	-2.752 ***	-3.002 ***
Unknown origin	-0.004	-0.001	0.001	-0.001	-0.006	-0.006	-0.006	-0.005	-0.003
share	2.240 ***	2.097 ***	2.048 ***	2.102 ***	2.263 ***	2.225 ***	2.202 ***	2.168 ***	2.116 ***
Others	-0.010 **	-0.011 **	-0.005	0.003	0.007	0.006	-0.005	-0.005	-0.018 **
share	0.631	0.655	0.509	0.289	0.222	0.286	0.417	0.405	0.472
Time dummies:					*yes*				
Controls:					*yes*				

Notes: *** p<0.01; **p<0.05; *p<0.1; Table shows the results of changing population in a specific neighborhood in Berlin; dependent variable is logarithmized rental prices per sqm; fixed-effect panel regression with robust standard errors

Table 13) Results for the Difference-in-Difference Fixed-Effects Estimation of Apartment Prices on Positive Treatments. Source: Own Illustration.

Dependent Variable: Logs of Apartment Prices									
Change in %	>0	>0.01	>0.05	>0.1	>0.15	>0.2	>0.25	>0.3	>0.4
All migrants	-0.001	-0.009	-0.018 **	-0.017	-0.027 *	-0.049 **	-0.020	-0.039	-0.021
share	0.031	0.047	0.084	0.063	0.099	0.190	0.079	0.104	0.058
Arabs	-0.006	-0.001	0.000	-0.002	-0.006	-0.005	-0.004	-0.001	-0.019 **
share	0.355	0.304	0.286	0.320	0.356	0.348	0.327	0.293	0.485
Turkish	0.024 ***	0.024 ***	0.025 ***	0.022 ***	0.019 **	0.012	0.016	0.012	0.006
share	-4.473 ***	-4.422 ***	-4.439 ***	-4.302 ***	-4.130 ***	-4.031 ***	-4.026 ***	-3.983 ***	-3.939 ***
Polish	-0.008	-0.007	-0.008	0.000	0.005	0.000	0.006	0.005	0.024
share	-2.116	-2.151	-2.208	-2.566	-2.708	-2.574	-2.651	-2.616	-2.703 *
EU-13	-0.022 ***	-0.025 ***	-0.033 ***	-0.032 ***	-0.035 ***	-0.027 **	-0.045 ***	-0.057 ***	-0.071 **
share	2.315 **	2.386 **	2.571 ***	2.421 ***	2.297 **	2.142 **	2.189 **	2.131 **	2.037 **
EU-15	-0.022 ***	-0.024 ***	-0.016 **	-0.013 *	-0.012	-0.010	-0.002	-0.023	-0.013
share	4.021 ***	4.059 ***	3.773 ***	3.610 ***	3.494 ***	3.448 ***	3.366 ***	3.506 ***	3.419 ***
Soviet Union	0.011	0.015 *	0.009	0.014 *	0.011	0.014	0.006	0.005	0.008
share	-3.261 **	-3.468 **	-3.169 **	-3.310 **	-3.069 **	-3.076 **	-2.789 **	-2.759 **	-2.764 **
Yugoslavia	0.011	0.014 *	0.019 **	0.020 **	0.025 ***	0.019 *	0.022 **	0.026 **	0.010
share	-4.275 ***	-4.393 ***	-4.599 ***	-4.582 ***	-4.597 ***	-4.373 ***	-4.401 ***	-4.465 ***	-4.010 ***
Unknown origin	-0.006	-0.007	-0.007	0.001	0.001	0.000	-0.003	-0.008	0.004
share	1.969	2.033	2.028	1.689	1.681	1.713	1.769	1.853	1.655
Others	-0.009	-0.010	-0.013	-0.014 *	-0.014	-0.028 **	-0.021	-0.034 *	-0.026
share	0.390	0.414	0.524	0.526	0.429	0.512	0.320	0.337	0.292
Time dummies:					*yes*				
Controls:					*yes*				

Notes: *** p<0.01; **p<0.05; *p<0.1; Table shows the results of changing population in a specific neighborhood in Berlin; dependent variable is logarithmized apartment prices per sqm; fixed-effect panel regression with robust standard errors

Apartment prices

The results for apartment prices show patterns similar to those of rental prices. For thresholds of >5%, >15% and >20%, prices decrease by 1.8%, 2.7%, and 4.9%, respectively. Arab migrants have a negative impact for the >40% threshold (1.9%), whereas all other thresholds do not show significant results. Parallel to what was observed for rental prices, Turkish migrants appear to positively impact apartment prices if the number of Turkish migrants increases. The thresholds from >0 to >15% all have significant coefficients between 2.4% and 1.9%. There are similar effects for Soviet Union migrants and Yugoslavians. Their coefficients range between 1.4% and 1.5% and between 1.4% and 2.6%, respectively. It is also noteworthy that the shares of migrants from Turkey, the former Soviet Union and the former Yugoslavia are highly negatively correlated with the prices. This likely indicates an enclave building within the city. Therefore, a demand shift could cause the prices to increase faster assuming a relatively inelastic supply.

The results for Polish migrants are not statistically significant, while the results for EU-13 and EU-15 countries show highly negative effects on prices. The EU-13 results show the strongest evidence of a negative relationship because all thresholds show statistically significant negative effects. The effect increases from the >0% threshold to the >40% from 2.2% to 7.1%, which follows the expectation that the size of the effect will increase for higher thresholds. For EU-15 migrants there are negative effects for apartment prices for the >0%, >1%, >5% and >10% thresholds, with decreasing effect sizes from 2.2% to 1.3%. The share of EU-15 migrants is positively correlated with apartment prices, which is difficult to interpret as pointed out earlier.

To check for robustness, we run the same analysis not only for positive changes, but also for negative ones; the results are shown in Appendix B. In principle, an impact should be observed for positive and negative changes, but with opposite signs because, if migrants are perceived as a disamenity, then areas with decreasing migrants should become more attractive to natives and, if demand decreases, prices should also decrease. Hence, for negative changes we expect positive impacts for those groups that have negative impacts and vice versa. The results in Appendix B show that the thresholds differ but that the directions of the coefficients are, as expected, opposite in sign to the results with positive changes in Tables 10 and 11.

3.6 Discussion

The first part of the analysis successfully replicates the results of Accetturo et. al (2014), Braakman (Braakmann, 2019) Sá (2015) and uses the shift-share instrumental variable approach by Card (2001). The results show a negative impact of migrants on housing prices as well as a similar effect on rental prices. The instrument decouples long and short-term immigration effects and indicates short-term negative effect of immigration on the development of prices in local real estate markets. This provides support to the theory that an increase in consumption of urban amenities by immigrants leads to outmigration of local population, which results in lower prices. Controlling for the ethnic background of immigrant groups, the results show different impacts on housing prices and rents. While migrants from Arab countries tend to negatively impact both apartment and rental prices, EU-migrants appear to have positive effects on rental prices. These results suggest that, depending on cultural background and education level, immigration may have opposing effects on real estate markets.

The results of Part II fail to identify a fixed "tipping" point for any group of migrants, but the dynamics of migration influence and the impact on rental and apartment prices are becoming more transparent as the changes differ in terms of threshold and migration group. Some results can be explained by the observed relationship from Part I that an increase of migration in a relatively short period of time has the character of a disamenity. This applies to the increase in the Arab population. But for some groups, such as the Turkish, the one from Yugoslavia and the former Soviet Union, an alternative explanation is necessary because the coefficients indicate an effect that is opposite in direction to what is expected. The unexpected sign may be caused by past 'balkanization' (Frey, 1995). Figure 3 shows, as an example, the geographic distribution of Arab and Turkish migrants in the city of Berlin, which is indicative of pull factors to cultural proximity (see Appendix B for the figures for other groups). When there are significant shifts in dominant local population groups, there is a synchronous movement of real estate prices to the change of this migration group. This is due to a demand shift under the assumption of relatively inelastic supply, which causes an increase in prices. Short-term negative market shifts due to a disruption of the composition of the native population in the individual neighbourhoods already occurred at the time of the past migration wave.[28] Additional immigration from the same cultural background is incorporated as additional demand, as the native population, in this case the already residing inhabitants, including the past immigrants, are not seeing additional immigration from the same group as a disamenity and, therefore, do not value the city quarter differently. Here a native outcrowding is unlikely.

The negative impact of additional EU-migration seems to validate this hypothesis. As additional immigration from both EU-15 and EU-13 countries are causing a short-term price decline parallel to additional immigration from Arab countries. The cultural difference between both immigrant groups indicates that the cultural background is not the decisive factor, but the simple timing of immigration and the valuation of amenities of the dominant native population in the individual neighbourhoods (Accetturo et al., 2014; Borjas, 2005; Mussa, Nwaogu, & Pozo, 2017).[29] The demographic shock of unexpectedly high immigration from these countries during our observation period is causing negative market reactions. The critique of Jaeger et. al. (2017) that a significant change in immigration composition is necessary to distinguish clearly between short-term and long-term effects of immigration can therefore be supported.

However, to identify a clear pattern of the price impact of immigration, our dataset has some omitted-variable limitations. Further socio-demographic data of education and financial background of both native and immigrant population is necessary to control for the interaction between social classes, as well as the interaction between cultural backgrounds. Moreover, English proficiency, as the common lingua franca, would indicate a common denominator.

---

28 See Chapter 2 for the historic overview of immigration waves to the Federal Republic of Germany.

29 The contradicting results of EU-immigration in Part I and Part II is likely due to the timing in our dataset. While the EU-migration wave occurred at the beginning of our panel, positive long-term effects on rental prices in Part I are already included, outweighing the short-term price decline indicated in Part II.

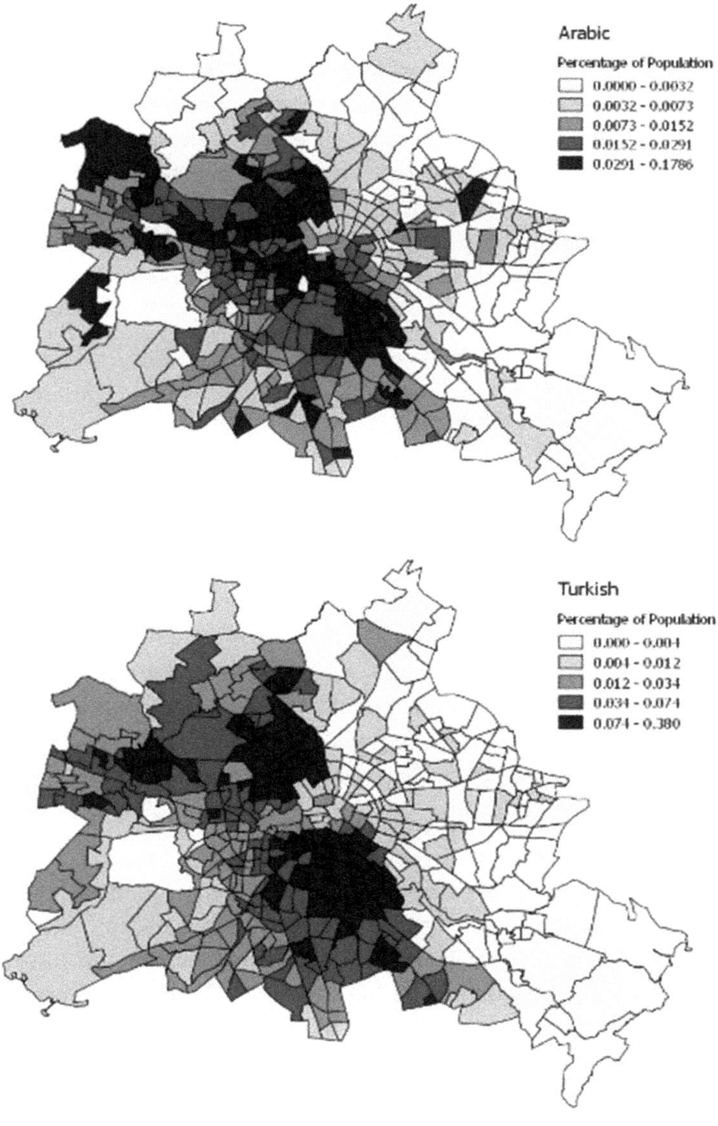

Figure 8) Spatial Distribution of Arab and Turkish Migrants across Berlin. Source: Own Illustration.

Fischer (2012), Frey (1995) and Borjas (2005) argue that enclave building tendencies are due to different cultural backgrounds and mostly language barriers. Unfortunately, further socio-demographic data on this granular level is currently not available in Germany. Moreover, research on spatial dependency and a longer timeframe of datasets on several major cities are necessary to derive a common pattern of the long and short-term effects of immigration on the German real estate market. A general problem of research on immigration and house prices is that the relationship between the two opposing price effects of increased demand and diminishing perceived local amenities for the native population is not clearly quantifiable. This problem has not yet been adequately addressed in the scientific community.

3.7 Conclusion

This paper identifies the effects of immigration on housing prices in the largest German city, Berlin. The dataset consists of a five-year panel for 447 comparable neighbourhoods that are relatively homogenous in terms of socio-demographic characteristics. We use a fixed-effects methodology and incorporate 'shift-share' instrumental variables. Our results indicate a short-term negative relationship between the inflow of migrants on housing prices and rents. Furthermore, the analysis supports the claim of native outmigration due to an immigration shock. However, controlling for the cultural background and countries-of-origin of the individual immigrant groups, the relationship appears more complex.

Using a fixed-effects difference-in-differences methodology to identify a "tipping" point, the estimation controls for an absorption rate of migrants in real estate submarkets, depending on the magnitude of immigration. While a tipping point cannot be identified, the results indicate different market reactions of various migrant groups depending on the size of the change and the population composition of the individual neighbourhoods. In cases where enclaves are present an increase in migrants from comparable background is likely to cause an increase in prices due to a demand shift. Yet, in places where no enclaves can be identified, an immigration shock causes a native outflow as the result of the change of consumption of local amenities, which leads to a price decline. As these market reactions are consistent over several cultural backgrounds, the paper concludes that in case of changing migrant composition the country-of-origin is not the predominant factor causing market shifts, but the timing of immigration and long-term demographic adaption processes in city quarters are likely the key drivers. The results indicate that a differentiating between migrants and the composition of the absorbing markets is necessary to portray the complex relationship between housing prices and immigration.

4 The Impact of Crime on Residential Real Estate Prices in Hamburg, Germany

4.1 Introduction

The economic impact of crime has been the subject of many studies during the past decades. Generally, the motivation to investigate this topic is due to the fundamental responsibility of governments to provide security to its citizens. Intuitively, public safety is the basis for modern societies to prosper and to ensure economic activity. A company, for example, will only be able to produce something if its property is not robbed and its employees are safe on their way to work. Most societies delegate this responsibility for safety to public authorities. The authorities' legitimacy strongly depends on the ability to ensure public safety. If governments fail to provide safety, individuals must provide for their own safety through other means; consequently, they may not accept the government collecting taxes. As resources are scarce, policy makers have a strong interest in spending money to ensure public safety in the most efficient way; it is, therefore, studied thoroughly in most countries.

However, the nature of public safety poses several difficulties to policymakers and to researchers analysing its impact on economic activity. Safety is measured through the absence of crime, which is a public service provided by the government in deterring crime by police work, for example. A common strategy is to measure the impact of crime implicitly by estimating housing prices. Hedonic modelling allows one to include crime measures as variables in regressions. Many studies have been conducted in this way and have raised several issues regarding the validity of these models. One major concern when estimating the economic impact of crime is the endogenous nature of crime measures as comprehensively pointed out by Ihlanfeldt and Mayok (2010).

In this paper, we exploit a six-year panel data set reaching from 2012 to 2017 containing prices for apartments and single-family homes and crime data on Hamburg's city quarter level investigating the relationship between crime and housing prices. We use the fixed-effect panel data methodology to analyse the impact of different crime measures. Due to the absence of exogeneous instrumental variables, we further implement a dynamic panel data approach to deal with the endogeneity of crime. The results indicate a weak relationship between

J. de Graaff, *Essays on the Impact of Urban (Dis-)Amenities on the German Real Estate Market*, Essays in Real Estate Research 18,
https://doi.org/10.1007/978-3-658-31623-5_4

violent crime and apartment prices. In more general terms, the results further underscore the difficulties to analyse the impact of crime given that it is endogenous.

The paper is structured as follows. First, a brief summary is provided of (a) the relevant literature and (b) the potential problems of analysing the impact of crime that result from the endogeneity of crime. Second, the data set and the empirical strategy are presented. After analysing the results and discussing the findings, we provide a brief conclusion.

4.2 Literature Review

Empirical research about the impact of crime on urban development has been part of the literature since the late 1960s. The first economic model by Becker and Ehrlich (1968) interpreted crime as a trade-off between the expected gains from conducting a crime and the chance of being convicted. Since then, crime has been in the focus of research in urban economics and real estate alike.

Neighbourhoods change in the long-term as a result of the many socio-economic developments that happen inside and outside of the neighbourhood. Changing crime levels are often an early indicator of such developments. Typically, crime levels are quickly capitalized into housing prices due to the important role they play in choosing a location to live. As Dugan (1999) and Morenoff et al. (2001) show, urban residents tend to move to different, safer neighbourhoods as soon as their perception regarding the crime level changes. Additionally, Cullen and Levitt (1999) identify a difference between the willingness to move based on the average income of a neighbourhood. According to their study, higher income households tend to move much quicker than poorer households, which likely leads to a further concentration of poverty and a lowering of the attractiveness of an area.

Numerous studies, mostly on US datasets, have shown that the changing of household preferences due to crime has an impact on housing prices. For example, Rizzo (1979) finds evidence for Chicago, using a 5-year dataset on the neighbourhood level, that various crime types have significant negative effects on house prices. Gibbons (2004) also investigates the effect of different crime types on house prices for a 3-year panel data set of London and uncovers a negative impact of vandalism, but no statistically significant effect of burglary. Buck et al. (1993) find mixed results on a 14-year data set depending on the type of specification of the empirical models. A more recent study by Tita et al. (2006) also uses a panel data set containing data from 1995-1998 for Columbus, Ohio. The empirical evidence indicates the capitalization of crime into the housing markets depending on the income level of the respective neighbourhoods. Hence, short-term capitalization of crime into housing markets on the neighbourhood level shows sufficient empirical potential to be further investigated.

According to Ihlanfeldt and Mayok (2010), 18 papers researched the relationship between housing prices and crime empirically. Although one or two additional papers need to be considered, they provide a good overview of the empirics on this topic. The papers tend to be divided into two main categories: whether the authors treat crime as an exogeneous or endogenous variable and whether the data is organized in panel-data, cross-sectional, or time-series data format. Furthermore, one must consider the literature that analyses non-US data sets separately as differences in culture might have an impact, too.

Most of the empirical papers treat crime as an exogeneous variable and do not address the issue of endogeneity of crime.[30] The endogeneity of crime can potentially result from several sources. Firstly, a positive relationship between crime and house prices can be expected for high income neighbourhoods as they are likely to attract criminals because of their expectation to generate higher payoffs. Hence, it is likely that expensive neighbourhoods attract certain criminals such as burglars. Secondly, criminologist know that crime is reported with higher accuracy in wealthier neighbourhoods (Langworthy, 1999). This might result in an upward bias between house prices and the incidence of crime because of the higher accuracy of crime measurement in higher priced neighbourhoods. Thirdly, special characteristics of the building or the area might attract burglars or drug consumers. Especially wealthy areas with large and representative buildings might attract burglars because they assume that the expected payoff of breaking

30 The papers are: Gray and Joelson (1979), Thaler (1977), Hellmann and Naroff (1980), Dubin and Goodman (1982), Clark and Cosgrove (1990) , Taylor (1995), Case and Mayer (1996), Bowes and Ihlanfeldt (2001), Lynch and Rasmussen (2001), Schwartz et al. (2003), and Braakmann (2016).

in is higher than in other areas or buildings. But neither the properties of the buildings nor the associated crimes may be measured or collected in the analysed data sets resulting in an omitted variable bias. Fourthly, higher income households might be able to protect themselves against crime better than lower income households. This would result in a downward bias of the incidence of crime in expensive neighbourhoods, counteracting the higher attractiveness of higher income neighbourhoods to criminals (Eide, Aasness, & Skjerpen, 1994). Finally, criminologist know that people tend to commit most crimes in their personal surrounding, which could result in an upward bias for lower income neighbourhoods (Repetto, 1974; Pope, 1980). Therefore, crime is highly endogenous and needs to be treated as such.

The papers treating crime as endogenous usually apply instrumental variable approaches to overcome this issue. Gibbons (2004) uses commercial crime densities and distances to the nearest area of nightlife as instruments arguing that alcohol is strongly correlated with violent crime. Bottoms and Wiles (1997) provide evidence that the closing time of nightlife areas and the amount of crime are highly correlated. Ihlanfeldt and Mayock (2010) adapt this approach and use the square footage of several commercial land use categories to instrument crimes assuming that other land-uses have a similar effect on crime as nightlife. Burnell (1988) and Rizzo (1979) deal with the endogeneity problem using numerous socio-economic, demographic and fiscal variables as instruments. Cornwell and Trumbull (1994) use tax revenue per capita among others. The rationale is that areas with greater interest in law enforcement will vote for higher taxes to strengthen the police force. An additional approach is introduced by Tita et al. (2006). They use the murder rate as an instrument arguing that murder is the most precisely reported crime and is according to Fox and Zawitz (2007) significantly correlated to violent crime. One issue with most instruments is the lack of proof of the validity of the instruments, as Ihlanfeldt and Mayock (2010) point out. Gibbons (2004) and Ihlanfeldt and Mayock (2010) validate their instruments, which would make it attractive to use a similar approach in this paper. However, the uniqueness of their data sets inhibits an adoption and makes different strategies necessary.

Most papers are based on US data sets. Few relevant papers focus on other regions, such as Gibbons (2004) on London. A classical Becker/Ehrlich-deterrence model is applied by Entorf and Spengler (2000) on a state level data set of Germany. However, their models differ to a certain extent from the approach of this paper as their dependent variable is not the house price but the crime rate. Other Becker/Ehrlich deterrence models are done by Carcolici and Uberti (2009) on a province level for Italy and by Han et al. (2013) and Braakmann (2016) for England and Wales.

4.3 Data

Hamburg is a city in northern Germany with approximately 1.8 million inhabitants in 2019. The data are available on an annual basis from 2012 to 2017 and contain prices for apartments and single-family homes, crime measures, and socio-economic factors. The house prices are collected and aggregated on a city quarter level by a local valuation firm. They are based on actual transaction data. Overall, apartment prices are available for 60 city quarters, while single-family house values are available for only 36 city quarters. The difference is due to different land uses across city quarters: Some city quarters are dominated by multi-family homes, others by single-family homes. Therefore, not all city quarters show enough sales of single-family homes or apartment prices to aggregate to a reliable average price. Furthermore, some city quarters have prices for apartments only, some for single-family homes only and some for both.

Initially, we will run regressions to estimate the impact of crime on home prices separately for single-family homes and apartments. Later, we will combine the data on both single-family homes and apartments in a single regression to check for the robustness of the estimates. The prices will serve as the dependent variables and are transformed with the natural logarithm to account for outliers.

The crime data are provided by the publicly available Hamburg Police statistics, which are reported annually and contain the most important crime categories. The data include 9 individual crime measures (robbery on streets and public places, aggravated assault, burglary, car theft, shoplifting, damage to property, crime against asylum law, consumption of drugs, and drug distribution) and 4 aggregated crime categories: total crimes, total robbery, total assault, and total theft. It is important to mention that some crime measures double count crimes. For example, total robbery includes robbery on streets and public places already. Therefore, not all crime measures can be included in the models at the same time due to the danger of collinearity. Furthermore, some crime measures are related to transportation hubs, such as the Hamburg harbour, and are not relevant in the context of house prices. After considering their relevance for house prices and adjusting for double counting, the following seven crime measures will be considered: total robbery, total assault, total theft, burglary, car theft, drug consumption, and property damage.

As is common practice in previous research, the different crime categories are further aggregated into property and violent crime measures. The reasoning is that violent crimes may affect people's decision to live in a certain neighbourhood differently from property crimes. In fact, previous research shows that violent crimes, such as assault, have a stronger impact on property prices than property crimes, such as burglary. This indicates that it is not the crime type per se that matters for location decisions, but the psychological effect or perception of personal safety associated with the crime level in a certain area. Henceforth, aggregation allows us to account for the general crime level in an area and not only one particular type of crime. However, the empirical strategy involves both approaches and we will estimate the impact of both aggregate crime levels and individual types of crime.

As crimes are committed by people and the number of people plays an important role when evaluating absolute crime figures, crime is generally defined in terms of crimes per inhabitants or the crime rate. The main argument is that the chance of being a victimized is higher if the crimes committed per person is higher. Yet, criminologists have argued that the number of crimes is driven not only by the number of residents, but also by the amount of business activity, which is not captured by the typical definition of the crime rate. Bowes and Ihlanfeldt (2001) suggest yet another definition of the crime rate: crimes per acre. They provide evidence in the context of housing prices that such a measure of the crime density is more meaningful and yields effects than the standard crime rate. Ihlanfeldt and Mayok (2010) build on these findings and identify the crime density as the measure with the highest explanatory power[31]. Therefore, we will also use two

31 They use simple OLS to identify which of three measures has the highest explanatory power in their case. They use level, rate and density and generate R^2 values of 0.317, 0.353, and 0.385.

definitions of the crime rate, one relating crimes to the number of inhabitants and one relating crimes to square kilometres of area.

Numerous control variables are included in the data set. These are retrieved from the statistical bureau of the City of Hamburg. The controls are reported on an annual basis on a city quarter level and include: the unemployment rate, average income per taxpayer, and population density. Previous research showed that unemployment and crime are highly correlated. Some studies find evidence that mainly property crime is triggered by unemployment (Janko & Popli, 2015), but others find a broader relationship between all crimes and unemployment (Fagan & Freeman, 1999). Furthermore, criminologists have identified different effects of crime on households depending on their wealth. Poorer neighbourhoods tend to suffer more from violent crime than richer neighbourhoods (Tita et al., 2006). Hence, the estimations of this paper control for unemployment *(unemployment_rate)* and income *(income_per_tax_payer)*. Unfortunately, no data is available for the distribution of age and gender in the city quarters, which does not allow to control for young males, which would be also an important socio-demographic factor influencing crime (Baier & Pfeiffer, 2007). Furthermore, the estimation uses the population density *(pop_density)* as a proxy for the level of urbanity to account for differences in the development of urbanity during the observation period of the city quarter (Glaeser et al., 2001). The reason is that the level of urbanity catches many developments in terms of changes in urban amenities that could have occurred during the observation period but cannot be controlled for by the fixed effects. Hence, controlling for population density should reduce the omitted variable bias. A summary of all variables is provided in Table 1.

However, their crime rate does not account for population changes because the population in the respective area is only available for the base year.

Table 14) Summary Statistics. Source: Own Illustration

Variable		Obs	Mean	Std. Dev.	Min	Max	Description
Apartment price		360	3,814.42	1,003.16	1,893.26	7,021.51	Price per sqm for apartments in €
Single-family home price		216	3,328.97	783.50	2,129.39	6,499.22	Price per sqm for single-family homes in €
Aggregated price		426	3,677.37	1,004.34	1,893.26	7,021.51	Aggregated prices of apartments and sfh in €
Area		426	7.39	6.51	0.57	35.39	Area of each city quarter in square km
Population		426	23,208.30	16,160.43	1,281.00	91,703.00	Number of people per city quarter
All crimes comitted		426	2,282.44	1,771.50	120.00	8,300.00	Total number of crimes registered in each city quarter
	rate	426	112.78	123.46	10.29	1,115.51	Total number of crimes per 1000 inhabitants
	density	426	511.22	464.43	4.18	2,093.66	Total number of crimes per square kilometer
Violent Crimes		426	232.21	207.67	4.00	1,114.00	Violent crimes registered in each city quarter
	rate	426	10.68	11.18	0.90	118.58	
	density	426	48.55	45.81	0.23	209.50	
Property Crimes		426	1,839.74	1,392.27	42.00	6,335.00	Property crimes registered in each city quarter
	rate	426	88.17	79.75	3.58	753.46	
	density	426	413.80	375.21	1.46	1,570.22	
Robbery		426	22.33	23.23	0.00	149.00	Robbery registered in each city quarter
	rate	426	1.00	1.24	0.00	12.90	
	density	426	4.85	5.68	0.00	36.35	
Assault		426	207.11	184.38	4.00	1,000.00	Assaults registered in each city quarter
	rate	426	9.55	10.04	0.90	111.25	
	density	426	43.12	40.30	0.23	195.31	
Theft		426	1,158.68	880.06	24.00	3,846.00	Total thefts registered in each city quarter
	rate	426	56.51	54.90	2.05	486.96	
	density	426	268.68	253.32	0.81	988.00	
Burglary		426	91.55	71.11	0.00	495.00	Burglary registered in each city quarter
	rate	426	4.13	1.80	0.00	10.79	
	density	426	18.19	13.42	0.00	75.65	
Car theft		426	26.32	19.76	0.00	111.00	Car theft registered in each city quarter
	rate	426	1.36	1.37	0.00	14.26	
	density	426	6.45	6.62	0.00	34.60	
Drug consumption		426	46.97	44.00	0.00	232.00	Drug consumptions registered in each city quarter
	rate	426	2.64	5.54	0.00	73.56	
	density	426	10.40	11.98	0.00	69.39	
Property damage		426	228.06	169.04	7.00	884.00	Property damage registered in each city quarter
	rate	426	10.63	8.50	0.59	85.17	
	density	426	48.37	40.00	0.24	161.92	
Unemployment rate		426	5.00	2.25	0.90	10.76	Reported unemployment rate in %
Population density		426	4,962.25	4,205.32	135.00	19,014.49	People per square kilometer
Income per tax payer		426	42,144.19	24,515.30	18,172.00	170,408.00	Income per tax payer in €

4.4 Empirical Strategy

In regression models of the hedonic price type various characteristics of the neighbourhood and of the properties themselves are regressed on the sales prices of the individual properties. As our data set contains values of characteristics and prices that are aggregated by city quarter and year, the idiosyncratic properties of individual single-family homes and apartments are not captured. Yet, the strongly balanced panel structure of our dataset allows us to use a standard fixed-effect estimator to identify the relationship between crime and housing prices.[32] The fixed-effects estimator controls for all time-invariant characteristics of each city quarter. That includes, for example, all locational characteristics, such as distance to the CBD or the Elbe River, or access to local or long-distance transportation. As our panel has few time series observations (years 2013 to 2017) but many cross-section observations (city quarters), the underlying assumption is that no long-term structural changes happened during our observation period. This includes large infrastructure projects or substantial changes in quarter-specific policies. In case of Hamburg, this appears plausible as no major decisions regarding structural changes of the city were made during the observation period.[33] Our socio-economic control variables account for short-term changes in the size and structure of the population. The fixed-effects regression will have the form:

$$\begin{aligned} Y_{it} = {} & \beta_1 V_{it} + \beta_2 V_{it-1} + \beta_3 V_{it-2} + \beta_4 P_{it} + \beta_5 P_{it-1} + \beta_6 P_{it-2} + \cdots \\ & + \beta_k C_{k,it} + d_t + a_i + e_{it} \end{aligned} \tag{11}$$

where Y_{it} is the dependent variable of city quarter i in year t. β_1 is the coefficient of the violent crime rate V_{it} of city quarter i in t_0, β_2 is the coefficient of the violent crime rate V_{it-1} of city quarter i in t_{-1} and β_3 for V_{it-2} of t_{-2} respectively. P_{it} represents the property crime rate of city quarte i in t_0 and $P_{it-1,\, t-2}$ in t_{-1} and t_{-2}.

32 A Hausman-test indicated that the fixed-effect estimator should be preferred over the random effects estimator..

33 The government published a report about the development of Hamburg in 2018 for the period between 2011 to 2018. The major construction activities such as the construction of new city quarters (e.g. HafenCity, Graasbrook) took place before the observation period or after. Major announcements of structural changes took place only for the old train station of Altona. More difficult to assess are the programs implemented by politics to "improve" urban spaces.

The variables $C_{k,\, it}$ represents a vector of control variables, namely unemployment rate, the income per tax payer and the population density of city quarter i in year t. d_t represents time-dummies included to control for time fixed effects.[34] a_i represents the fixed-effects of each city quarter and e_{it} stands for the error term. The estimations will be executed with standard errors robust to heteroskedasticity and clustered on a city-quarter level. All calculations and procedures are done in *Stata*.

The endogenous nature of crime violates the strict exogeneity assumption of the fixed-effect estimator (Wooldridge, 2002, p. 265). As described above, crime is subject to at least five sources of endogeneity. The straightforward way to deal with this issue would be to apply an instrumental variable approach for all crime measures. Unfortunately, the dataset does not contain any variables that could be used as instruments. Additionally, it would be a difficult task to obtain the number of instruments needed for all seven crime measures. Several studies regress the crime measures separately and generate exact identification of the equations by using the same instrument for each measure. However, if crime varies over time and impacts housing prices, then all crime measures are likely to have an impact at the same time and should be included in one equation. Tita et al. (2006), however, use the murder rate as an instrument for violent crime and property crime rates in separate equations. Other studies using instrumental variables, such as Gibbons (2004) and Ihlanfeldt and Mayock (2010), have further dimensions in their data set to exploit as instruments, which this data set does not have.

A further methodological issue is the dynamic nature of real estate prices and serial correlation in the error term. It is likely that real estate prices in period t depend on prices observed in previous periods. It is unlikely that prices fluctuate independently every year. This applies in particular in our case, where the prices are aggregated on the level of a city quarter. On this level, prices will likely be autocorrelated because they absorb all the properties of the respective city quarter and translate into a willingness to pay by the people conducting the transac-

34 These account for year-specific changes that affect all quarters, such as policy changes that apply to Hamburg in general and not just to individual city quarters.

tions. Therefore, autocorrelation of the residual is likely be an issue and needs to be addressed methodically. The most widely applied way to address this issue, is to include one or more lagged dependent variables into the equation:

$$Y_{it} = \gamma Y_{it-1} + \beta_{1,it} X_{1,it} \dots + \beta_k X_{k,it} + d_t + a_i + e_{it} \tag{12}$$

where Y_{it-1} is the lagged dependent variable and γ the autoregressive term of first order.

The dynamic panel data approach (DPD) raises estimation issues of its own. In particular, the fixed-effects estimator (i.e. the within transformation) produces inconsistent estimators in dynamic models. The unobserved time-invariant characteristics (e.g. fixed-effects) of the city quarters are correlated with the regressors and are part of the error term. As Y_{it} and Y_{it-1} depend on the fixed effects a_i, Y_{i-1} is correlated with the error e_{it}. By subtracting the individual's mean value of Y and the other regressors, the within transformation creates a correlation that is not distributed independently from the error term. The commonly known Nickell bias is a serious issue when using the within estimator in dynamic panels. Nickell (1981) pointed out that the inconsistency of β_k approaches $1/T$ as N approaches infinity. As our panel is relatively short and has a relatively large number of cross-section units, using an estimator that provides consistent estimates is necessary.

Given potential autocorrelation of the error term, we estimate a dynamic panel data (DPD) model using the generalized methods of moments (GMM) methodology popularized by Arellano & Bond (1991). The transformation of the data outlined by Arellano & Bover (1995) is usually referred to as "forward orthogonal deviations" or "orthogonal deviations". The idea is to transform the data to remove the fixed-effects that correlate with the lagged dependent variable. The easiest transformation is to take first differences of the data, that is, subtract the previous observation from the contemporaneous one to remove the fixed effects of the equation. This procedure works well with balanced panels for which no observations are missing. Orthogonal deviations do not difference consecutive observations but subtract the average of all future available observations from the contemporaneous one, which allows for gaps in the data set. As we have a strongly balanced panel, we will additionally estimate the first-difference estimator for robustness.

Roodman (2009) laid out several criteria of data sets for which this methodology is suitable: panels with small T and large N; a linear functional relationship; one dependent dynamic variable, which depends on its own past values; independent variables that are not strictly exogeneous, fixed individual effects, heteroskedasticity and autocorrelation within individual errors but not across them. As discussed above, all the outlined criteria are fulfilled for the current data set. The data set contains 60 panel units observed over 6 time periods; the price data are most likely dynamic; the crime data are endogenous for several reasons; the Hausman-test suggests a fixed-effects setting; we can expect at least first-order autocorrelation.

The GMM estimator includes lagged dependent variables as shown in equation 12 but accounts for the correlation between the fixed-effects and the lagged dependent variable through a set of instrumental variables.

Summarizing the empirical strategy, firstly we apply standard fixed-effects methodology ignoring the dynamic nature of the apartment prices and endogeneity issues. Secondly, the system GMM estimator will be used to account for the dynamic behaviour of the price data. Therefore, we treat our dependent variables as dynamic and include one lagged dependent variable into the equation. Time-dummies (time fixed effects) are included to absorb changes that affect the city in general and, therefore, cause correlations across the individual city quarters. We use standard errors that are robust to heteroskedasticity. Due to the sample size of our data set the lag specification needs to account for instrument proliferation, which means that too many instruments are generated for the sample size. Several strategies are included in the applied procedure *xtabond2* in *Stata*. One is to collapse the instrument matrix by using the option "collapse" for the GMM-style instruments. A further strategy is to restrict the use of certain lagged variables as instruments to reduce their number. The implementation of the procedure requires some "trial-and-error" as it is crucial to define the number of lags and how the lagged variable is treated. Roodman (2009) recommends to report as many specifications as possible and to check for robustness changing the lag specifications.[35]

We estimate two models separately for the apartment prices and the single-family homes. Furthermore, we first estimate models for the two main categories of crime, namely violent and property crime, and then individual models for the single crime categories. It is likely that real estate markets react with a time-lag on changes in the crime levels. Therefore, we include lags of the explanatory variables. Ihlanfeldt and Mayock (2010) find that significant effects can be observed for the third and fourth lag. The criminologists Vélez, Lyons, and Boursaw (2012) find evidence for a time lag of two years for violent crime. Although the empirical research suggests that longer lags might be necessary to obtain significant results, we will include two lags of the crime measures in order to maintain a sample of sufficient size.

The fixed-effects model without the dynamic estimator is given as follows:

$$\begin{aligned}\ln(price)_{it} = {} & \beta_1 violent\_crime_{i,t} + \beta_2 violent\_crime_{i,t-1} + \\ & + \beta_3 violent\_crime_{i,t-2} + \beta_4 property\_crime_{i,t} \\ & + \beta_5 property\_crime_{i,t-1} + \beta_6 property\_crime_{i,t-2} \\ & + \beta_7 unemployment\_rate_{it} \\ & + \beta_8 population\_density_{it} + \beta_9 income_{it} + d_t + a_i \\ & + \varepsilon_{it} \end{aligned} \tag{13}$$

for $i = 1$ to 60 city quarters, $t=1$ to 6 years. *ln(price)* is the logarithm of either apartment prices or single-family home prices per year t in city quarter i, *violent_crime* is the crime measure for all violent crimes, *property_crime* for all property crimes included with three lags. The *unemployment_rate*, *population_density* and *income* control for important socio-economic properties that might have changed over time and influence prices. The term a_i represent the individual fixed-effects and the e_{it} is the error term.

The dynamic model adds lagged dependent variables and instruments theses:

35 The full syntax of the Stata command can be found in the Appendix; we will apply several specifications to check for robustness of the model.

$$\begin{aligned}\ln(price)_{it} = {} & \beta_1 \ln(price)_{it-1} + \beta_2 violent\_crime_{i,t} \\ & + \beta_3 violent\_crime_{i,t-1} \\ & + \beta_4 violent\_crime_{i,t-2} + \beta_5 property\_crime_{i,t} \\ & + \beta_6 property\_crime_{i,t-1} + \beta_7 property\_crime_{i,t-2} \\ & + \beta_8 unemployment\_rate_{it} \\ & + \beta_9 population\_density_{it} + \beta_{10} income_{it} + d_t \\ & + a_i + \varepsilon_{it}\end{aligned} \tag{14}$$

Both equations are also estimated for the individual crimes.

4.5 Results

The empirical results are presented in Table 15 and Table 16. Overall, the results show weak evidence for a negative relationship between housing prices and crime. The aggregated crime measures show no significant results for the fixed-effects estimation at all. However, the GMM estimator shows significant effects for both violent and property crime for apartment prices. The violent crime rate has negative and statistically significant effects for t_0 and t_{-2}. In particular, the coefficients indicate that for a 1 percentage point -increase in the violent crime rate, say from a rate of 11% to 12%, apartment prices decrease by 0.5% in t_0 and by 1.03% in t_{-2}. Similarly, a 1 percentage point increase in the property crime rate, say from 88% to 89%, decreases apartment prices by 0.23% in t_{-1}. As is common in models with consecutive lags of the driving variable, crime rates in our case, the estimation results also show some positive coefficients, for example for the violent-crime rate at t_{-1} and for the property crime rate at t_0. To smooth out the erratic results for consecutive coefficients, it helps to calculate the implied long-run impact of the driving variable, crime in our case, on the dependent variable, house or apartment prices. To obtain the long-run impact we use the standard time series method of dividing the sum of the crime coefficients at the different lags by one minus the sum of the coefficients of the lagged dependent variable. For the GMM estimator of the apartment price equation reported in Table 15, the long-run impact of the violent crime-rate on apartment prices is:

$$\frac{-0.0052 + 0.0092 - 0.0103}{1 - 0.554} = -0.014. \tag{15}$$

Given that the mean value of the violent crime rate is 10.68 (Table 14), a unit increase in this rate is approximately equal to a 10% increase in the violent crime rate. We can, therefore, conclude that, in the long run, a 10% increase in the violent crime rate will lower apartment prices by 1.4%. The equivalent calculations for the property crime rate are

$$\frac{0.0012 - 0.0023 + 0.0005}{1 - 0.554} = -0.0014. \tag{16}$$

Given that the mean value of the property crime rate is 88.17 (Table 14), a 9 unit increase in this rate is approximately equal to a 10% increase in the property crime rate. We conclude that, in the long run, a 10% increase in the property crime rate will lower apartment prices about 1.3% $(-0.0014 * 9 = 0.0126)$. Hence, a 10% increase in the property crime rate lowers apartment prices only slightly less than a 10% increase in the rate of violent crime. Property crime and violent crime have about the same impact on apartment prices. Earlier research shows to the contrary that property crime plays a lesser role with regards to house prices than violent crime (Bowes & Ihlanfeldt, 2001; Braakmann, 2016; Tita et al., 2006).

It is apparent from Table 15 that the aggregate crime measures do not have statistically significant impact on the prices of single-family homes. This applies regardless of whether the static or dynamic fixed-effects estimator is employed. A potential reason lies in the fact that far fewer observations are available for the estimation of the single-family home regressions than for the apartment regressions.

Splitting the aggregate crime measures into its components does not in general yield statistically significant results for the impact of crime on prices (Table 16). There are no statistically significant results at all for the GMM estimators with lagged dependent variable. There is some statistical significance recorded in Table 16 for the static fixed-effects models, but the results are consistently significant across apartments and houses only for burglaries. For robberies there is a noticeable economic impact only for single-family houses. We will focus our discussion again on the long-run impact.

We consider first the case of robbery and its impact on single-family homes. Absent a lagged dependent variable, the long-run impact can be derived as the sum of the distributed lag coefficients,

$$0.0177 - 0.0116 - 0.0274 = -0.0213. \tag{17}$$

According to Table 14, the robbery rate is low at 1. A unit increase in this rate would amount to a doubling of the robbery rate.[36] Such a doubling would reduce single-family home prices by 2.1% in the long run. A look at the individual coefficients of the robbery variable suggests that a rise in the robbery rate takes some years to materialize. Statistical significance arises only with a two-year lag. In the light of this fact and the observation that there appears to be a pattern in the coefficients from positive over slightly negative to significantly negative, one could make the reasonable argument that the long run impact of increased robbery is represented solely by the coefficient of robbery at lag 2, which is -0.0274. That would raise the long-run impact from -2.1%, as calculated above to - 2.7% for a doubling of the robbery rate.

There is no distinct pattern in the coefficients for burglary, either for apartments or for single-family homes. Therefore, calculating the long-run impact appears sensible. For the long-run unit impact of burglaries on apartment prices we find

$$-0.0070 + 0.0059 - 0.0033 = -0.0044, \tag{18}$$

which is a price discount of a little less than one half of one percent. For burglaries, a unit increase in the burglary rate amounts to a percentage increase in the burglary rate of 24% given a mean value of 4.13 for the burglary rate according to Table 14. This is a reasonable increase as it is less than one standard deviation of the burglary rate as recorded in Table 14.

36 Although a doubling of the rate may sound as a strong assumption, it is in effect rather reasonable given the small base level of robberies: all it takes is a change in the number of robberies equal to its standard deviation (Table 14). To assume changes of a magnitude equal to a standard deviation are common practice in empirical work.

Table 15) Fixed-Effects and Dynamic GMM Regression of Aggregated Crime Figures on Apartment Prices and Single-Family Home Prices. Standard Errors Robust to Heteroskedasticity. Source: Own Illustration.

Dependent Variable	log of apartment prices		log of single family homes	
	FE	GMM	FE	GMM
log of dependent variable				
t-1		0.5540 **		1.1900 ***
		(0.04)		(0.00)
Violent crime rate				
t	-0.0024	-0.0052 ***	-0.0014	0.0008
	(0.16)	(0.00)	(0.38)	(0.58)
t-1	0.0011	0.0092 **	-0.0027	-0.0077
	(0.60)	(0.02)	(0.52)	(0.21)
t-2	-0.0031	-0.0103 **	0.0007	0.0017
	(0.37)	(0.01)	(0.64)	(0.49)
Property crime rate				
t	0.0005	0.0012 **	-0.0003	-0.0009
	(0.15)	(0.02)	(0.62)	(0.40)
t-1	-0.0003	-0.0023 **	-0.0002	-0.0010
	(0.42)	(0.03)	(0.76)	(0.50)
t-2	-0.0004	0.0005	-0.0004	-0.0004
	(0.41)	(0.50)	(0.46)	(0.73)
Controls	Yes	Yes	Yes	Yes
Time Dummies	Yes	Yes	Yes	Yes
N	240	180	144	108
Instruments	-	25	-	28
R^2	0.801	-	0.767	-
AR(1) (p)	-	0.039	-	0.013
AR(2) (p)	-	0.296	-	0.931
Hansen (p)	-	0.179	-	0.813
Sargan (p)	-	0.019	-	0.17

* p<0.1, ** p<0.05, *** p<0.01; Robust standard errors

Table 16) Fixed-Effects and Dynamic GMM Regression of Specific Crime Figures on Apartment Prices and Single-Family Home Prices. Standard Errors Robust to Heteroskedasticity. Source: Own Illustration.

Dependent Variable	log of apartment prices		log of single family homes	
	FE	GMM	FE	GMM
log of dependent variable				
t-1		0 8840 **		0.1160
		(0.01)		(0.91)
Robbery				
t	0.0111	0.0410	0.0177	0.0086
	(0.39)	(0.50)	(0.34)	(0.89)
t-1	0.0001	-0.0269	-0.0116	0.0392
	(1.00)	(0.52)	(0.58)	(0.74)
t-2	-0.0036	-0.0021	-0.0274 *	0.0038
	(0.70)	(0.94)	(0.05)	(0.93)
Assault				
t	-0.0032	0.0034	-0.0010	-0.0024
	(0.18)	(0.64)	(0.81)	(0.77)
t-1	0.0016	0.0068	-0.0031	0.0046
	(0.52)	(0.32)	(0.50)	(0.83)
t-2	-0.0043	0.0007	0.0071	0.0049
	(0.26)	(0.94)	(0.14)	(0.82)
Theft				
t	0.0015 *	0.0007	-0.0012	-0.0046
	(0.08)	(0.73)	(0.16)	(0.28)
t-1	-0.0008	-0.0038	0.0014	0.0019
	(0.29)	(0.15)	(0.25)	(0.64)
t-2	-0.0008	-0.0031	0.0009	0.0014
	(0.41)	(0.62)	(0.45)	(0.83)
Burglary				
t	-0.0070 *	0.0157	-0.0039	0.0037
	(0.08)	(0.17)	(0.47)	(0.78)
t-1	0.0059 *	0.0123	-0.0094 *	-0.0100
	(0.10)	(0.56)	(0.06)	(0.36)
t-2	-0.0033	0.0104	-0.0039	0.0090
	(0.48)	(0.58)	(0.26)	(0.36)
Car theft				
t	-0.0033	-0.0018	0.0275	0.0585
	(0.75)	(0.98)	(0.11)	(0.37)
t-1	-0.0055	0.0161	0.0188	0.0656
	(0.53)	(0.46)	(0.12)	(0.29)
t-2	0.0027	0.0148	-0.0197	-0.0030
	(0.80)	(0.80)	(0.30)	(0.93)

Dependent Variable	log of apartment prices		log of single family homes	
	Fixed Effects	GMM	Fixed Effects	GMM
Drug consumption				
t	0.0020	-0.0120	0.0085	0.0391
	(0.80)	(0.71)	(0.38)	(0.47)
t-1	0.0006	0.0104	0.0064	0.0008
	(0.92)	(0.77)	(0.21)	(0.97)
t-2	0.0080	-0.0068	0.0029	-0.0077
	(0.23)	(0.84)	(0.46)	(0.45)
Property damage				
t	0.0017	0.0041	-0.0017	-0.0056
	(0.40)	(0.63)	(0.61)	(0.50)
t-1	0.0007	0.0028	0.0036	-0.0103
	(0.68)	(0.77)	(0.24)	(0.57)
t-2	-0.0001	0.0035	0.0012	-0.0012
	(0.95)	(0.66)	(0.60)	(0.90)
Controls	Yes	Yes	Yes	Yes
Time Dummies	Yes	Yes	Yes	Yes
N	240	180	144	108
Instruments	-	40	-	43
R^2	0.819	-	0.835	-
AR(1) (p)	-	0.039	-	0.5
AR(2) (p)	-	0.694	-	0.633
Hansen (p)	-	0.119	-	0.797
Sargan (p)	-	0.019	-	0.064

* p<0.1, ** p<0.05, *** p<0.01; Robust standard errors

The long-run impact of a unit rise in the burglary rate on single-family home prices is given as,

$$-0.0039 - 0.0094 - 0.0039 = -0.0172, \quad (19)$$

which is a price discount of 1.7%. The impact of a rise in the burglary rate on single-family homes is very significantly larger than on apartment prices. One reason could be the demographic differences among single-family homeowners and people that live in apartments. The psychological effects of burglary on victims might cause homeowners to move faster and base their decision on where to move more on the danger of burglary. For example, people that live in single-family homes might have more children on average and might therefore be more sensitive to burglars. A second reason could be that people living in single-family homes are on average wealthier and experience higher losses if burglary happens. This might lead to a stronger reaction in areas where burglary occurs more often. A reaction could be the moving away or selling of the house, which would then put pressure on prices and would lead to a stronger decrease in prices.

4.6 Robustness & Further Investigation

There are two possible explanations for the absence of robust significant results in the fixed-effects estimations in section 4.5. Either the model equations are misspecified or there simply is not a relationship that is similar to previous research embedded in our data set. To be able to conclude the latter, we need to take a closer look at potential misspecifications of our models.

The quality criteria of our dynamic panel estimations look reasonably robust. The AR(1) and AR(2) tests indicate the presence of first-order autocorrelation and the absence of a higher-order autocorrelation. This is expected from a statistically sound model. Therefore, including one lagged dependent variable seems reasonable in the presence of autocorrelation. Furthermore, the Hansen-p statistic does not indicate instrument proliferation. The Hansen-p statistic is above the 10% level for all models estimates, which suggests that the number of instruments is not too high. However, Roodman (2009) recommends reducing the number of instruments as far as possible even if the Hansen-p values appear fine.

On another note, the general specification of including two lags of the crime measures may cause a problem. From an economic point of view, it is reasonable to expect a delay between criminal activities and a potential impact on prices. It is difficult, however, to argue how long it might take to influence prices. As stated earlier, Ihlanfeld & Mayock (2010) identify impacts on prices in t_{-3} and t_{-4} for robbery and assault. One issue with the present data set is that the sample size will be reduced to $n=120$ if four lags are included. Additionally, including all lags at a time might create multicollinearity among the crime measures, which will be further discussed in section 4.6.1. Hence, regressing only one lag at the time might produce better results.

Table 17 shows the fixed-effect estimation of the violent crime rate and the property crime rate on apartment prices using one lag at a time. The estimations rule of thumb because the model uses two crime measure variables with two time lags and three control variables and three time dummy variables, which adds up to 12 explanatory variables in total. However, the basis for this rule of thumb is unknown and not backed by empirical evidence, but merely based on experience.

In comparison to other studies, our data is small. The data set contains 60 panel units over a time span of 6 years (n=360) for the apartment prices and even fewer for the single-family home prices. Running regressions combining both price measures leads to 71 city quarters over 6 years ($n = 426$). More recent studies that investigate the relationship between housing markets and crime, such as Braakmann (2016) or Kim (2018), use data sets containing 1.8 million and 150.000 observations, respectively. Older studies have sample sizes in the tens of thousands, such as Tita et al. (2006) or Gibbons (2004). Only Ihlanfeldt & Mayock (2010) use a comparably small data set of $n = 502$ and find a significant relationship. Yet, according to the rule of thumb presented above, their minimum sample size would have been 3,500 as their regression includes 7 crime variables with 4 lags. Their results, however, are robust and show a significant relationship between housing prices and robbery and assault[37] using a much smaller sample size as the rule of thumb recommends.

Green (1991) and Maxwell (2000) both investigated the minimum sample size for multivariate regressions. Green (1991) derives a rule of thumb by not only taking the number of variables into account but also the required explanatory power and the confidence level. For an explanatory power of $R^2 = 80\%$ and significance at the 5%-level he recommends using at least $N = 104 + m$ observations. This would translate into a minimum sample size of 112 for the basic fixed-effects model. Maxwell (2000) derives a minimum sample size from the average correlation between the predictor variables and between the dependent and independent variables. Maxwell suggests that the larger the correlation among the independent variables the larger the sample must be; vice versa for the correlation between the independent and the dependent variables. The issue here is that in the case of our data set the predictors are highly correlated among

37 Ihlanfeldt & Mayock (2010) also use an instrumental variable approach and do not only regress the crime measures with housing prices.

each other. The correlation between the violent crime and property crime is 0.91, while the correlation between the apartment prices and the two crime types is of medium size -0.36. This shows that sample size would be an issue according to Maxwell (2000), because for an average correlation level and 5 predictors 419 observations would be considered the minimum acceptable number. Hence, the strong correlation among the predictors and the small sample size might contribute to the largely insignificant relationship between crime and housing prices.

Near Multicollinearity

Multicollinearity is often an issue for social-science and economics because variables that concern people's behaviour or the environment are likely correlated with each other. The fixed-effects estimator already controls for time-invariant characteristics of the panel participants, which makes it possible to include far less variables than if one were using cross-sectional estimators and that reduces the risk of multicollinearity. Furthermore, multicollinearity is, at least theoretically, only an issue regarding the explanatory power and does not affect the consistency of the estimator. That is, why some researchers do not worry too much about it. In practice, however, multicollinearity can alter the size of an impact and potentially bias the coefficients, which can explain the absence of significance. The procedures implemented in *Stata* automatically exclude variables that show perfect collinearity. But near multicollinear variables remain in the estimation. For study designs trying to quantify the effect of certain variables, such as this one, it is an issue that is difficult to solve.

A standard procedure to analyse the presence of near multicollinearity is measuring the variance inflation factors (VIFs). The VIFs show which coefficients are likely affected by the presence of multicollinearity. The higher the VIF the more likely multicollinearity is an issue. The mean VIF for the crime variables is 7.28, which is well above the commonly accepted threshold of 2.50. Only burglary is below the threshold and seems to be relatively uncorrelated with the other crime measures. See the Appendix C for a detailed representation of the VIFs of the estimations above.

A likely source of multicollinearity for our data is that different crime categories are correlated with each other. Areas with significant criminal activity typically have a high rate of criminal behaviour not only in one crime category but of many or most at the same time.

The good news is that OLS estimators remain consistent in the presence of high collinearity. The bad news is that standard errors will be inflated, and it will be harder to detect significant relationships. The confidence intervals tend to be very wide and t-statistics very small. Hence, the size of an impact needs to be very large to be detected. Furthermore, the results tend to be very unstable from one regression to another depending on the included variables and their relationship. If two variables are positively correlated, their coefficients tend to be negatively correlated. This means that a different sample might produce different results, because an overestimate of one parameter may underestimate the other.

The following outlines strategies to deal with multicollinearity. First, one needs to exclude sources such as the misspecification of the data. Second, it is preferable to increase the sample size. Third, sometimes separate variables are just representations of the same construct. In this case, one could combine variables that measure the same thing into one variable. The aggregation of the individual crime types to the violent crimes and property crimes should already account to a certain extend for multicollinearity among the crime types. Fourth, sometimes it helps to perform joint significance tests of the variables instead of t-tests for variables individually. See Appendix C for detailed results. The joint significant tests show that for the separated crime measures show significant values for the GMM estimation as well when jointly tested. Hence, the aggregated significance of crime is also found in the GMM estimation leading to the conclusion that aggregated crime measures might work better.

A fifth strategy is to drop highly correlated explanatory variables from the model. For example, Tita et al. (2006) and Entorf and Spengler (2000) do not include all crime measures in the same model, but estimate a separate regression for each crime measure. As described above, this might produce omitted variable bias if research suggests that certain variables belong in the model. Yet, one could argue that due to the high correlation among the crime categories the separate estimation might produce better results. For this reason, the following shows three fixed-effect regressions with only one crime measure at the same time. The results indicate no improvement in terms of significance and effect size (Table 19) as no significant relationships can be identified.

Table 19) Fixed-Effect Regressions with the Separate Estimation of Aggregated Crime Measures with Robust Standard Errors on Apartment Prices. Source: Own Illustration

		Total Crime	Violent Crime	Property Crime
Crime rate		-0.0001	-0.0007	0.0001
		(0.57)	(0.51)	(0.79)
	t-1	0.0000	-0.0001	0.0000
		(0.63)	(0.96)	(0.88)
	t-2	-0.0001	-0.0027	-0.0006
		(0.65)	(0.40)	(0.28)
Controls		Yes	Yes	Yes
Time Dummies		Yes	Yes	Yes
N		240	240	240
R-sq		0.795	0.796	0.797
AIC		-943.4	-944.8	-946.1

* p<0.1, ** p<0.05, *** p<0.01; Robust standard errors

Lag Specification

The lag distribution of the models in section 2.5 is chosen because of Vélez, Lyons and Boursaw (2012) and the empirical findings by Ihlanfeldt and Mayock (2010), who use 2 and 4 lags in their estimation, respectively. The above discussion provides good arguments why lags are necessary. The main argument is that there is a time lag between an area becoming more criminal and people knowing about that. However, Ihlanfeldt and Mayock (2010) provide little information about the length of the time lag. In distributed lag models, the choice of how many lags should be employed is a difficult one because theory will not reveal how long it takes for information to spread. Hence, empirical strategies can be employed to identify the exact number of lags that are necessary. The issue at hand with the data set in this paper is the limited number of observations as already discussed extensively. But, one strategy of identifying the best lag structure might be to check out alternative lag specifications.

Three strategies are usually employed when identifying the exact lag length in models where empirical findings or theory suggest lagged explanatory variables[38]. The first strategy is to check the different setups for statistical significance. Usually one would include the maximum number of lags and reduce the lags stepwise to remove lags that are not statistically significant. The second strategy involves the application of information criteria designed to measure the goodness of fit of a model, with the model fit being discounted by the number of included variables. The Akaike Information Criterion (AIK) and the Schwartz Bayesian information criterion (SBIC) are the two most commonly used ones. The decision rule for both criteria is: the smaller the criterion the more preferred the model. The third strategy analyses the residuals for the presence of autocorrelation.[39]

Strategies for Dealing with Endogeneity

Real exogeneity is rare. For crime, the sources of endogeneity are manifold, which requires a strategy for dealing with it. Many studies do not do that, and this study uses a fixed-effect estimation that neglects the endogeneity of crime as well. Recent studies that account for the endogeneity of crime tend to have unique data sets that make it feasible to implement instrumental variable strategies. But these are hardly replicable in general. Gibbons (2004), for example, uses distances to the nearest nightlife area or wine bar and commercial crime densities. This requires that the data set allows one to determine an exact location of the house and the crimes committed in the neighbourhood. Ihlanfeldt & Mayock (2010) also use a unique instrumentation strategy. They employ the changes in 26 commercial land use categories to generate a full set of 52 instruments. This allows them to instrument not only the crime measures at t-0 but also all lagged variables in their regression. Unfortunately, our data set lacks the necessary variables. Firstly, the granularity of the data does not allow for any useful

38 The implementation of a dynamic estimator is of course relevant in our case as well. The determination whether to include one or more lagged dependent variables is done based on the test by Arellano and Bond (1991).

39 Examples for tests of this sort are the Breusch-Godfrey LM test or Box-Ljung Q test.

spatial lags or distance calculations. Secondly, there is no other data like the one Ihlanfeldt & Mayock (2010) had available.

The general issue with the instrumental variables approaches is the identification of enough instruments. Having one instrument will not be enough for the current study due to the multiple predictors that would require suitable instruments. Other studies help themselves on this issue by estimating the crime measures individually and not simultaneously. Entorf & Spengler (2000) do that with similar data for the federal states in Germany but do not take endogeneity into account. Tita et al. (2006) estimate total crime, violent crime and property crime and separately instrument them with the murder rate. The argument is that murder solves most sources of endogeneity, such as measurement error. However, estimating the crime categories separately would likely create an omitted variable bias, which produces inaccurate coefficients.

Granularity of the Data

Connected to the issue of endogeneity is the granularity of the data set. The 60 panel units cover a land area of 7.4 km² on average and inhabit 23.208 people. The reported crimes can be geographically allocated only on a city quarter level and not on a street level, as in other studies. This is due to the reporting conventions of the publicly available statistics. The statistical offices do not report street-level data or even geo-coded data of this kind. Similarly, the data provider collects transaction prices and aggregates them on a city quarter level. Fortunately, both data sets can be combined because the socio-economic control variables, the price data and crime data are available for the same spatial units. This is not something that can be assumed to hold for other cities. It is not the case, for example, for Frankfurt am Main or Cologne. For example, Cologne issues a variety of statistics and reports the same crime figures as Hamburg. However, the geographical units for the crime variables are different from the units of the socio-economic variables. To the author's best knowledge, the present data set is the most granular data set that is available for any German city. This, of course, does not bode well for empirical research on German data.

Intuition suggests that granularity of data is an important concept when it comes to crime. The differences between streets and areas in terms of crime and the decision where to live sometimes changes in very short distances from one street to the next. Furthermore, the empirical evidence suggests that street-level data yields the best model results. All papers that yield significant relationships between crime and housing prices use geocoded or street-level data, except for one that uses aggregated data on the level of the federal states.

4.7.2 General Limitations of the Study

Observation period

The observation period of the data set stretches from 2012 to 2017. In the context of real estate prices in Germany, this period is characterized by one of the strongest real estate price increases Germany ever experienced since reliable data became available. Figure 9 shows the development of residential real estate prices between 1975 and 2018. The index is corrected for inflation and therefore in real terms. Germany experienced a decrease in real residential real estate prices in the early 1980s and, again, from 1995 to 2010. From then on, real estate prices have increased on a continual basis, comparable in speed only with the rise in the late 1970s. For all of the years considered in this study, the German residential real estate market has been in a strong upward movement. Looking at the Hamburg market, the increases are even stronger than that for Germany in general during the observation period (Figure 10). This is in accordance with current market reports that identify the large agglomeration areas as the drivers behind the recent real estate boom in Germany.

The reasons for the real estate boom in Germany are manifold and would require an analysis of its own. However, one commonly accepted cause is ECB's expansionary monetary policy, which is captured by the very low or zero interest rates since 2010 (Figure 9). The main financing rate of the Euro-system decreased in the aftermath of the fiscal crisis of 2008 and the concurring financial turmoil of European countries.

The fact that the observation period of this paper is during the phase where German real estate prices in general and cities such as Hamburg in particular experienced the strongest increases in recent history, means that, although an effect might be present, it may be particularly difficult to observable. Methodologically, the time-dummies (time fixed-effects) should catch any underlying time-trend. Furthermore, the lagged dependent variable in the GMM-estimation accounts for autocorrelation between consecutive periods. However, stronger, more important factors might overlay the crime-rate, if crime only has a small impact. The empirical results from other studies indicate that the effects of crime on prices tend to be relatively small even under more ordinary time periods of monetary policy. Tita et al. (2006, p. 310), for example, identify an short-run elasticity of -0.0002 for property crime levels and housing prices.

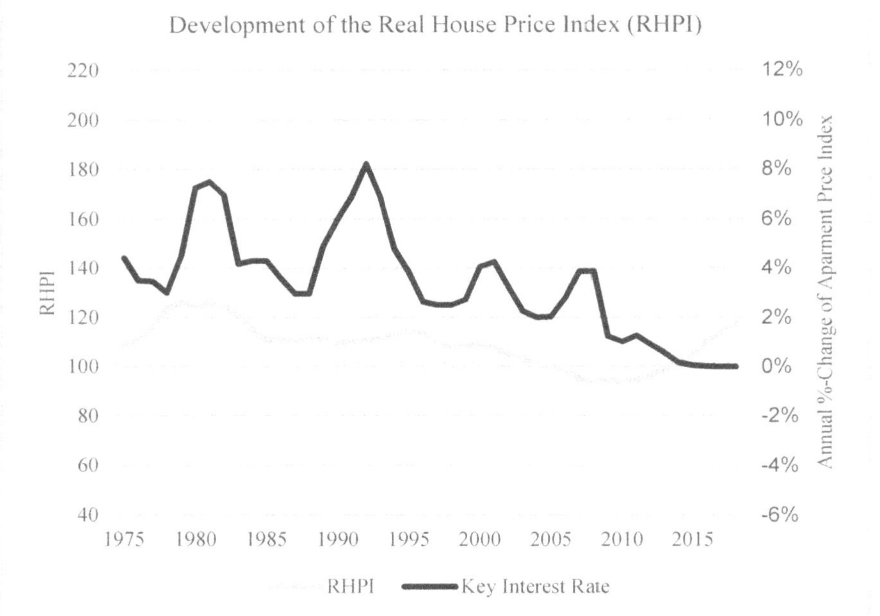

Figure 9) Development of the Real Residential Real Estate Prices in Germany Between 1975 and 2018.[40] Source of Data: Mack, Adrienne, and Enrique Martínez-García (2011); Fed Dallas (2019); ECB (2019)

40 Index: Real House Price Index. Key Interest Rate: Annual Average of the Monthly Key Interest Rate. Until December 1998 Discount Interest rate of the German Bundesbank, from January 2002 on Main Refinancing Rate of the European Central Bank.

Measurement of Crime

The measurement error of crime statistics may cause a discrepancy between the actual crimes committed, the measured crimes according to the official statistics, and the crime level perceived by the citizens living in the area or thinking about moving into or out of the area.

Figure 10) Development of the Residential Real Estate Prices in Hamburg for the Sample Period. Source: Own Illustration.

The measurement error is likely to bias the estimation results as mentioned above. The crime statistics will not capture all crimes because a) only crimes that the police are aware of are counted, b) different reporting patterns exist by the type of victim, as wealthier victims have a higher tendency to report the crime to the police c) the different intensity of police work, and d) changes over time in the way crime statistics are generated. For example, some crimes are reported more than others. Car theft, for example, is likely to have a reporting quota of close to 100% because most cars are insured against theft.

Any difference between the perception of crime and the actual crime rate may also impact the estimation results. The US Presidential Commission's Report (1967), for example, highlighted the devastating effects of violent crime in comparison to other crimes. Wilson (2013) concludes that crimes against what is perceived as personal safety are more threatening than other crimes. Intuition also suggests that property crimes have a different impact on people's perception of safety than for example assault.[41] Yet, more recent research suggests that the crime type does not alter the fear of crime, but that it is relatively unimportant which crimes happen in the area (Zhao, Lawton, & Longmire, 2015). More interestingly, people are aware of the criminal level of their direct surroundings. Zhao, Lawton and Longmire (2015) also find a relationship between the perception of crime and the actual reported crimes within a 528 feet radius. They further conclude that this relationship may explain why other studies have found significant relationships between fear of crime and crime on the neighbourhood level (Rountree, 1998; Schafer, Huebner, & Bynum, 2006; Wyant, 2008). However, they also note that the explanatory power is relatively small with R^2 between 20% and 22%. This might explain why the current study fails to identify a significant effect. First, the granularity is not sufficient to identify a relationship and the effects may be too marginal so that other more important effects overlay the relationship with crime. Nevertheless, Zhao, Lawton and Longmire (2015) support the findings of the economic literature that people are aware of the crime level in their neighbourhood. If that is the case, theory suggests that people would choose safer neighbourhoods, which would alter the demand and affect prices.

41 Burglary usually has a devastating effect on people, although it is a property crime. People, whose apartment has been broken into, report that they do not feel safe at home anymore and that they experience an invasion of their most private places.

Choice of subject (Hamburg market)

Although Hamburg is among the 10 cities in Germany with the most crime, the public considers Hamburg not as a major hotspot of crime. [42] The choice of Hamburg as the focal point of this study is based on data availability. However, considering the 20 largest independent cities in Germany, choosing Hamburg might not be the ideal subject to investigate the relationship between crime and housing prices. Firstly, Hamburg ranks 7th among the 20 largest cities in terms of the 5-year average of crimes per 10,000 inhabitants. The analysis of the city size and the crime per capita does not allow any conclusions whether larger cities are safer than smaller ones or not. Munich is the third largest city in Germany in terms of inhabitants but is the safest of the 20 largest ones. Additionally, Frankfurt am Main has the most crime activity, but only it is only the fifth largest city.

Regarding the relationship of housing prices and crime, Table 20 shows the average land values per square meter of 2017 as an indicator for the price level of each city. Frankfurt has modest land values compared to Munich or Düsseldorf. Berlin, however, is the city with the second highest level of criminal activity. But it also has high land values. Hamburg is in the middle of the 20 largest cities in Table 20, which also holds true for its per capita income and unemployment rate. Hence, Hamburg does not represent any extreme in the socio-economic spectrum of large cities and is, therefore, unlikely to be problematic as a research subject. Whether or not Hamburg is suitable is difficult to answer, but someone would expect that the effects become more visible in the data if crime is particularly high or prices are particularly low. Therefore, Hamburg might not show significant relationships because other factors are more important or because it is not one of the major concerns of people living in Hamburg or moving to Hamburg.

42 The author presented an abstract of this paper at the annual conference of the European Real Estate Society 2017. One comment from the audience was that, the commentator being Spanish, would not connotate crime with Hamburg but rather with other cities such as Paris, Marseille or in the case of Germany Berlin.

Table 20) Comparison of Selected Socio-Economic Variables of the 20 largest German Cities. Sources: Destatis (2019).

Rank	City	5y-average crime rate per 10k inhabitans 2013-2017	GDP/capita 2016	Unemploy-ment rate 2017	Youth unemploy-ment rate 2017	Population in 2017	Average Land Values per sqm 2017
1	Frankfurt a.M.	157.97	91,099 €	5.9	5.7	746,878	421 €
2	Berlin	153.71	36,798 €	9.0	9.6	3,613,495	695 €
3	Köln	141.52	59,407 €	8.4	5.6	1,080,394	461 €
4	Leipzig	140.19	35,123 €	7.7	8.2	581,980	265 €
5	Dortmund	135.28	36,781 €	11.1	9.7	586,600	219 €
6	Düsseldorf	133.12	79,619 €	7.4	5.8	617,280	1,691 €
7	Hamburg	132.51	62,793 €	6.8	5.6	1,830,584	655 €
8	Bremen	131.04	49,439 €	9.7	8.6	568,006	198 €
9	Dresden	116.04	37,993 €	6.6	6.4	551,072	171 €
10	Bonn	108.33	71,222 €	6.7	5.2	325,490	349 €
11	Duisburg	106.40	33,634 €	12.5	10.7	498,110	116 €
12	Essen	104.82	41,512 €	11.4	10.9	583,393	148 €
13	Karlsruhe	101.35	63,147 €	4.5	3.2	311,919	404 €
14	Wuppertal	101.20	37,186 €	9.3	9.0	353,590	126 €
15	Bochum	99.46	32,596 €	9.7	8.5	365,529	131 €
16	Stuttgart	96.61	82,397 €	4.7	3.1	632,743	957 €
17	Münster	96.51	56,612 €	5.4	3.8	313,559	217 €
18	Nürnberg	90.54	55,071 €	6.0	5.5	515,201	368 €
19	Bielefeld	82.54	38,588 €	8.3	7.0	332,552	193 €
20	München	77.43	75,186 €	4.2	2.7	1,456,039	2,533 €

Taking rental levels and rental changes into account, Hamburg ranks 4th place for average rental prices per square meter. Munich, which has the lowest rate of criminal activity, ranks 1st and Frankfurt, which has the highest rate of criminal activity, ranks 2nd. Again, taking other cities into account, there is no clear pattern visible at first sight, which suggests that a thorough analysis like the one of this paper is necessary to uncover a relationship or to arrive at the conclusion that the relationship plays a minor role for the German housing markets.

4.7.3 Propositions for Further Research

In summary, the limitations and shortcomings of the data set, the methodology and the properties of the research subject suggest the need for further research to gain additional insight. In the following, five propositions for further research are discussed. They intend to make it easier for future researchers who start their inquiry of the impact of crime on housing markets in Germany.

Proposition 1: Crime figures and price data need to be collected at a high level of granularity and within a coherent geographical framework.

Our comparisons to other studies revealed that data sets with data points on a more local level, i.e. more granular data, yield better results. This is especially true for the crime data because crime has a strong local impact on people's perception of crime and their actions with respect to buying or selling real property. The issue at hand is that geocoded crime figures are not publicly available for anywhere in Germany. Data collection is, therefore, dependent on the goodwill of the authorities to make this data available to research. The same holds true for the price data. Although data availability has improved due to online rental portals, the granularity of real transactions data is often available only commercially or not at all. Since data collection firms have identified data as a source of potential revenue in Germany, it is more difficult for researchers to obtain highly granular price data. Without knowledge of individual crime locations and prices and location data of individual real estate transactions, many methodological options are not available and will make robust findings unlikely in this particular context. This state of affairs is unfortunate both for researchers, who cannot pin down cause and effect in a reliable way, and for policy makers, who continue to rely on gut feeling in making decisions rather than on solid research.

Proposition 2: In the context of the relationship between crime and housing prices, small panel sizes prohibit the application of the necessary specifications.

The GMM-estimator, which is the standard method for panel fixed-effects models with autocorrelation in the residuals, requires a highly flexible data set. As seen in this analysis, short panels are highly limited with regards to choosing the right lag distribution. Including one or more autoregressive terms will always exclude one or more periods from the panel. This might cause the sample size to drop too low so that the instruments generated from the lags outnumber the groups of the panel. Therefore, larger sample sizes and panel length improve the flexibility to find the correct lag specification.

Proposition 3: The observation period matters in terms of the expected results and should be chosen with caution.

The observation period should lie within a period that represents normal market behaviour. The German housing market is in an unprecedented state for the following reasons. The interest rates for financing real estate have never been lower in the post-war history. The reason lies not only but also in the ECB's expansionary monetary policy to deal with the Euro crisis. The low yields and the unfavourable state of European economies, such as Italy, Greece or France, made Germany a save heaven in the eyes of investors. Furthermore, German investors are searching for investment opportunities because of the low yields on saving accounts and quality government bonds. This results in increasing real estate prices and a massive yield compression especially in large agglomerations such as Hamburg. Therefore, the question is whether fundamentals, such as the crime rate, play an important enough role in the current macroeconomic environment or whether investors currently ignore fundamentals such as the relative level of criminal activity. In general, the literature indicates that a relationship exists between real estate prices and urban amenities, such as public services in the form of crime prevention. Yet, investors may neglect fundamental indicators due to the expectation of rising market prices. The follow up question that arises is, if this holds true for fundamentals other than crime; and if so, what does that mean with regards to a real estate price bubble.

Proposition 4: The impact of crime on housing prices might be relevant for one market but not relevant for another.

There is extraordinarily little empirical research regarding the relationship of crime and housing prices for the German market. Technically, only Entorf and Spengler (2000) provide empirical evidence on the level of federal states; but they do not deal with issues that later research discussed, such as endogeneity and the dynamic nature of the relationship between prices and crime. Other countries have sound empirical evidence that points toward a strong correlation between crime and housing prices. The evidence for US-data is sound and has been investigated thoroughly throughout the years. Recent research for South Korea (Kim & Lee, 2018), Nigeria (Abdullahi Alhassan Ahmed & Joseph Awoamim Yacim, 2018), and the UK (Braakmann, 2016; Gibbons, 2004) also show evidence that violent crime has an impact on real estate prices. One must note that the methodologies differ markedly across studies and that not all papers address the endogeneity issue. The reasons why researchers have not yet focused on Germany are unclear. One reason may be that Germany is a relatively safe country in OECD terms (OECD, 2015) and that crime has not been a primary issue in the eyes of the public. Only in recent years has this topic risen to the public's attention because of problems in the course of the influx of refugees and organised crime from migrant clans and the Italian mafia.

Proposition 5: Researchers should think of new data sources to analyse the relationship between crime and housing prices.

The unreliability of crime statistics is widely known and accepted. Periodic surveys attempt to measure the difference between measured crime, experienced crime, and actual crime (Birkel, Church, Hummelsheim-Doss, Leitgöb-Guzy, & Oberwittler, 2019). However, criminologists know for quite a while that there is no static relationship between committed crimes and measured crimes, with the exception of very few crimes, such as car theft and murder. Hence, the public statistics only represent the known part of criminal behaviour. The extent to which crime is measured depends on other variables, such as the social status of the victim, the type of crime, and the relationship between the victim and the delinquent. How to measure crime properly is an entire research strand that needs further attention to improve the results with respect to housing values. Surveys seem a promising source of information because they show a high correlation with the actual crime figures. This means that people are aware of the criminal level in the area they live according to Zhao, Lawton and Longmire (2015). Instead of relying on police statistics, survey data could be a more reliable source of crime measurement than police statistics.

4.8 Conclusion

The goal of the paper is to provide empirical evidence on the relationship between crime and residential housing prices for a large German city. The strategy involved a unique data set that contained different crime measures as well as housing price data for single-family homes and apartments for the years between 2012 and 2017. The panel structure of the data set makes it possible to apply fixed-effect estimation methodology, which allows one to control for all observed and unobserved time-invariant characteristics at the level of the individual panel data units, which are city quarters (*Stadtteile*) in our case.. The data set involved annual price data for 60 city quarters of the city of Hamburg for apartment prices and 36 city quarters for the single-family homes, each observed over 6 periods.

The estimation strategy follows approaches used in previous studies. In addition, the methodology makes use of a generalized method of moments approach to allow for a lagged response of prices to changes in criminal activity. All estimates are based on aggregated crime figures and individual crime types. Due to data constraints, all estimates involve a maximum lag of two years between a change in crime and housing prices.

The obtained results are ambiguous. On the one hand, long run effects can be found for property and violent crime rates and apartment prices. Contrary to earlier research, violent crime seems to play a similar role in the long run than property crime. In general, the results of other studies show a dominant role of violent crime. For the German market, the long run impact of both crime categories seems to be equally important. Furthermore, robbery and burglary show long run impacts on apartment prices and single-family home prices. The latter is only influenced by burglary whereas apartment prices are influenced by both in the long run. Similar relationships are obtained when changing the crime measure from the crime rate to the crime density. On the other hand, the empirical strategy to include lags of the independent variables as instruments in order to deal with the endogeneity of crime fails to produce robust results in the case of the separate crime types. The problem at hand is that endogeneity is a widely accepted problem when estimating the impact of crime on housing prices. Relying mainly on the fixed-effect results may produce biased results, which should not be overinterpreted.

A thorough investigation of potential reasons for the absence of widespread robust results, which is contrary to the findings from previous research, leads to the formulation of 5 propositions that future work on German data may want to consider. Firstly, higher granularity of crime data is required to find robust relationships on a micro-level because people tend to perceive crime in their immediate environment. City quarter level data covers too much space and people. Secondly, the observation period as well as the sample size needs to be sufficiently large to deal with methodological challenges such as the time lag between crime and housing prices. Thirdly, the observation period itself needs to be considered carefully because it is possible, as in the case of Hamburg, that it is within a time of extraordinary developments, which could bias the result.

Fourthly, the application of findings from other markets may not prove to be useful for Germany as the country appears to be different in terms of crime and housing prices than, for example, the UK or the US; this may explain the absence of a robust correlations. Lastly, the methodological strategies should be extended more towards the psychological effects of crime as these may play a large role for the demand pattern for housing.

Further research therefore should focus on obtaining better crime and price data on a more granular level for longer periods of time. This is also a request to policy makers to open up access to detailed (anonymized) crime data, as it is done in the US and the UK. Research using UK and US data sets has access to geocoded crime figures that can be allocated on a street level and combined at the same granularity with price data. Braakmann (2016), for example, could use over 1.5 million geocoded data points for England and Wales from detailed governmental surveys. Such transparency is recommended for the German market as well to analyse the relevance or irrelevance of crime for the demand for housing.

5 Summary, Practical Implications, and Further Research

The aim of this thesis is to contribute to the knowledge about the impact of urban (dis-)amenities. The thesis consists of three empirical papers that investigate a specific topic that has been present in recent public debate. The first paper focuses on the determination of the attractiveness of a location from a consumer's perspective. Due to the recent housing boom in Germany, this question is especially relevant for developers, investors, and occupiers when evaluating location qualities. The second paper focuses on the impact of migration on housing prices in a major city, namely Berlin. The public debate resulted from the mass migration during recent years which is often referred to as the *refugee crisis*. The question to be answered is whether measurable impacts on prices can be observed due to the influx of certain ethnicities. Thirdly, the public is concerned about the impact of crime on all levels of society. Hence, the third chapter involves the analysis whether crime impacts housing prices based on a data set of Hamburg, the second biggest city in Germany. The following summary provides a brief overview of all chapters of this thesis and adds practical implications that result from the findings of each chapter.

Chapter 2 investigates the relative importance of urban amenities when choosing the location of an apartment. Very often hedonic modelling is used to examine the impact of one or more urban amenities on real estate prices, which then is interpreted as the people's willingness to pay for certain location criteria. This chapter takes a different approach by applying a MCDM methodology called AHP. The AHP derives relative weights of a set of criteria by using pairwise comparisons. Mathematically, the relative weight vector is derived by solving an eigenvalue problem of the comparison matrix obtained by comparing the criteria against each other. The paper analyses survey data from 683 respondents living in Germany that were chosen representatively for gender, age, education, and federal state residency. In total, 17 urban amenities in four categories are compared by the respondents. After deriving the relative weight vector of the full sample, the sample is split into several subgroups to identify differences in location choice preferences. Demographic cohorts define the subgroups, better known as the *Silent Generation*, *Baby Boomer*, *Generations X*, *Y*, and *Z*. Furthermore, differences between city size, and Eastern and Western Germany are analysed. The main result is that natural amenities and shopping facilities play a

J. de Graaff, *Essays on the Impact of Urban (Dis-)Amenities on the German Real Estate Market*, Essays in Real Estate Research 18,
https://doi.org/10.1007/978-3-658-31623-5_5

dominant role for all subgroups in choosing a location. Furthermore, the *Silent Generation* and *Generation Z* prefer good public transportation access whereas the working generations *(Baby Boomer, X, and Y)* value the distance to work more than the other two generations. The differences between Eastern and Western Germany reveal the preference of Easter German residents to be near public transportation. Similarly, people from smaller towns prefer a good connection to long-distance traffic indicating that their need to move to other cities is higher than for residents of larger cities. The practical implication of these results is firstly to get a better understanding of which urban amenities are more important than others. Secondly, the results can help developers or investors to judge location quality depending on their strategy. For example, when constructing an elderly home, the subsample of the *Silent Generation* might be useful to weight the urban amenities at a certain location more precisely by using the derived weights in a scoring model.

Chapter 3 empirically investigates the impact of migration on housing prices and the native population in Berlin, Germany. Berlin, is Germany's largest city with a high share in immigrants. The panel data contains observations for 447 LORs, which are designed to represent homogeneous areas in terms of socio-economic properties. The variables include the number of migrants from different ethnic backgrounds and residential real estate prices for 2012 to 2017 on an annual basis. The data set is examined using fixed-effect regression with a shift-share instrumental variable in order to disentangle the network effects that existing migrant communities have on new migrants from the current migration. The results show a significant negative short-term impact of migration on prices in Berlin with different intensities on rental and apartment prices. Additionally, the native population decreases in the course of an increase of the migrant population. The second part of the chapter investigates if a tipping point can be identified that chanes the prices when a migration shock occurs. The question is if prices decrease when a certain threshold of migration within one year is exceeded. The results indicate that two contrary effects move the prices. For migrant groups with an already existing large community in an LOR, additional migration from these groups works as a demand shock and increases prices. Migrant groups without larger communities tend to compete for the consumption of urban amenities with the existing population, which eventually lowers the quality of an area and puts pressure on prices. Overall, the results indicate that an effect is observable, and policymakers need to be cautious when it comes to migration.

The practical implications lie in the acceptance that migration will have an impact on real estate prices and on the native population, thus, it should be of concern when taking decisions in this regard.

Finally, chapter 4 answers the question if crime influences housing prices by analysing a data set from a German city. The data set contains apartment price and single-family home data for 60 of the 104 city quarters of Hamburg, Germany. Furthermore, for each city quarter crime figures are available for the years between 2012 and 2017. The data is organized as a panel data set and examined by using fixed-effect and GMM methodology. The reason to apply GMM estimators is the widely known issues of endogeneity of crime. Several reasons are known to bias crime figures in both directions, which implies using an instrumental variable approach to deal with the endogeneity. Due to the absence of suitable instruments in the data set, the GMM estimator developed by Arellano and Bond (1991) generates instruments from lagged independent variables. Additionally, real estate prices are most likely autocorrelated, which is also dealt with by including lagged dependent variables in the estimator. Furthermore, crime is also likely to have an impact with a time lag because it will take time for information about the criminal activity within a city quarter to spread. The results show long run effects of violent and property crime rate on apartment prices using the GMM estimator. The effect size is almost identical, which contradicts previous research, mainly using US and UK data, where violent crime takes a dominant role in influencing prices. Furthermore, long run impacts can be observed for robbery and burglary on apartment prices and single-family home prices. However, the effects of burglary on single-family home prices is stronger than on apartment prices. One reason could be that homeowners are more sensible to intruders into their privacy. Secondly, single-family homeowners might be more sensitive in protecting their property, which would result in lower demand for single family houses in high burglary neighbourhoods. However, the fixed-effect and GMM results for the disaggregated crime measures do not yield robust results. Furthermore, the GMM results are very unstable when changing the specifications of the estimation. The reasons likely lie within the structure of the data and the general difficulties of evaluating crime. The comparable small sample size, near multicollinearity of the crime measures, and the lack of instruments to deal with endogeneity might bias the results and avoid robustness. Unfortunately, the data set does not allow for further methodological adjustments. Further issues might be that crime is not highly relevant for the German market during the observation period because of a strong residential real estate appreciation. Additionally, Hamburg might be a difficult subject to be examined because it is a relatively wealthy and safe city compared to Frankfurt or Berlin, for example. A lot of previous research deals with criminal hotspots such as New York City in the 1980s, or London in the past decade, which cannot be compared to the situation in Hamburg in terms of criminal activity. Hence, further research should focus on more criminal hotspots in Germany, such as Frankfurt or Berlin. Researchers should then focus on obtaining highly granular data sets, if possible on a street level. Furthermore, longer observation periods are recommendable because of the quite recent developments in the German residential market. The discussion remains if the question of crime is as relevant for the German market as for other foreign markets. Also, researchers should think about new data sources to identify criminal areas. Survey data or data from media coverage might be useful in identifying perceived crime instead of reported crime. In the end, the demand drives the housing prices and if people think that a respective area is very criminal, demand for housing might decrease. Hence, perception of crime might play a significant role in determining the effects of crime on housing prices and should be further investigated.

Reference List

Abdullahi Alhassan Ahmed, & Joseph Awoamim Yacim. (2018). The Hedonic Modelling of Rental Values of Properties in Nasarawa, Nigeria. *Journal of Civil Engineering and Architecture*, *12*(5), 382–390. https://doi.org/10.17265/1934-7359/2018.05.006

Accetturo, A., Manaresi, F., Mocetti, S., & Olivieri, E. (2014). Don't stand so close to me: The urban Impact of Immigration. *Regional Science and Urban Economics*, *45*(1), 45–56. https://doi.org/10.1016/j.regsciurbeco.2014.01.001

Ahlfeldt, G. M., & Mastro, A. (2012). Valuing iconic design : Frank Lloyd Wright architecture in Oak Park, Illinois. *Housing Studies*, *27*(8), 1079–1099. https://doi.org/10.1080/02673037.2012.728575

Akbari, A. H., & Aydede, Y. (2012). Effects of immigration on house prices in Canada. *Applied Economics*, *44*(13), 1645–1658. https://doi.org/10.1080/00036846.2010.548788

Anderson, S. T., & West, S. E. (2006). Open space , residential property values , and spatial context. *Regional Science and Urban Economics*, *36*, 773–789. https://doi.org/10.1016/j.regsciurbeco.2006.03.007

Arellano, M., & Bond, S. (1991). Some Tests of Specification for Panel Data: Monte Carlo Evidence and an Appliation to Employment Equations. *The Review of Economic Studies*, *58*(2), 277–297.

Arnold, D., Rottke, N. B., & Winter, R. (2017). *Wohnimmobilien - Lebenszyklus, Strategie, Transaktion* (1st ed.). https://doi.org/10.1007/978-3-658-05368-0

Baier, D., & Pfeiffer, C. (2007). *Gewalttätigkeit bei deutschen und nichtdeutschen Jugendlichen - Befunde der Schülerbefragung 2005 und Folgerungen für die Prävention*. (100), 55.

Baltagi, B. H. (2005). *Econometric Analysis of Panel Data* (3rd ed.). West Sussex: John Wiley and Sohns.

BAMF. (2016). *Aktuelle Zahlen zu Asyl*. https://doi.org/10.1097/QAD.0000000000001808

BAMF. (2018). *Aktuelle Zahlen zu Asyl*. Berlin.

Barreto, M. A., Frasure-Yokley, L., Vargas, E. D., & Wong, J. (2018). Best practices in collecting online data with Asian, Black, Latino, and White respondents: evidence from the 2016 Collaborative Multiracial Post-election Survey. *Politics, Groups, and Identities*, *6*(1), 171–180. https://doi.org/10.1080/21565503.2017.1419433

Bartel, A. P. (1989). Where Do the New U.S. Immigrants Live? *Journal of Labor Economics*, *7*(4), 371–391.

Becker, G. S. (1968). Crime and Punishment: An Economic Approach. In *Journal of Political Economy* (Vol. 76). https://doi.org/10.1086/259394

Bender, A., Din, A., Favarger, P., Hoesli, M., & Laakso, J. (1997). An Analysis of Perceptions Concerning the Environm ental Quality of Housing in Geneva. *Urban Studies*, *34*(3), 503–513.

Bender, A., Din, A., Hoesli, M., & Laakso, J. (1999). Environmental quality perceptions of urban commercial real estate. *Journal of Property Investment & Finance*, *17*(3), 280–297. https://doi.org/10.1108/14635789910270521

J. de Graaff, *Essays on the Impact of Urban (Dis-)Amenities on the German Real Estate Market*, Essays in Real Estate Research 18,
https://doi.org/10.1007/978-3-658-31623-5

Birkel, C., Church, D., Hummelsheim-Doss, D., Leitgöb-Guzy, N., & Oberwittler, D. (2019). Der Deutsche Viktimisierungssurvey 2017. In *Bundeskriminalamt*. Wiesbaden.

Borjas, G. J. (2005). *Native Internal Migration and the Labor Market Impact of Immigration* (No. 11610). Retrieved from http://www.nber.org/papers/w11610

Bottoms, A. E., & Wiles, P. (1997). Environmental criminology. In *The Oxford handbook of criminology* (pp. 620–656).

Bourassa, S. C., & Hendershott, P. H. (1995). Australian Capital City Real House Prices, 1979–1993. *Australian Economic Review*, *28*(3), 16–26. https://doi.org/10.1111/j.1467-8462.1995.tb00990.x

Bowes, D. R., & Ihlanfeldt, K. R. (2001). Identifying the Impacts of Rail Transit Stations on Residential Property Values. *Journal of Urban Economics*, *50*(1), 1–25. https://doi.org/10.1006/juec.2001.2214

Braakmann, N. (2016). The link between crime risk and property prices in England and Wales : Evidence from street-level data. *Urban Studies*, 1–18. https://doi.org/10.1177/0042098016634611

Braakmann, N. (2019). Immigration and the Property Market: Evidence from England and Wales. *Real Estate Economics*, *47*(2), 509–533. https://doi.org/10.1111/1540-6229.12151

Brücker, H., Hauptmann, A., & Vallizadeh, E. (2015). Flüchtlinge und andere Migranten am deutschen Arbeitsmarkt: Der Stand im September 2015. In *Aktuelle Berichte* (No. 14/2015). Retrieved from http://doku.iab.de/aktuell/2015/aktueller_bericht_1514.pdf

Buck, A. J., Hakim, S., & Spiegel, U. (1993). Endogenous Crime Victimization, Taxes, and Property Values. *Social Science Quarterly*, *74*(2), 334–348.

Burnell, J. D. (1988). Crime and Racial Composition in Contiguous Communities as Negative Externalities : Prejudiced Households ' Evaluation of Crime Rate and Segregation Nearby Reduces Housing Values and Tax Revenues. *The American Journal of Economics and Sociology*, *47*(2), 177–193.

Caldera Sánchez, A., & Andrews, D. (2011). The Evolution of Homeownership Rates in Selected OECD Countries: Demographic and Public Policy Influences. *OECD Journal: Economic Studies*, *2011*(1), 1–37. https://doi.org/10.1787/eco_studies-2011-5kg0vswqpmg2

Carcolici, M. F., & Uberti, T. E. (2009). Geographical distribution of crime in Italian provinces: a spatial econometric analysis. *Jahrbuch Für Regionalwissenschaft*, *29*, 1–28. https://doi.org/10.1007/s10037-008-0031-1

Card, D. (1997). *Immigrant Inflows, Native Outflows, and the Local Labor Market Impacts of Higher Immigration* (No. 5927). Cambridge.

Card, D. (2001). Immigrant Inflows, Native Outflows, and the Local Labor Market Impacts of Higher Immigration. *Journal of Labor Economics*, *19*(1), 22–64. https://doi.org/10.1086/209979

Card, D., Mas, A., & Rothstein, J. (2008). Tipping and the Dynamics of Segregation. *The Quarterly Journal of Economics*, *123*(1), 177–218.

Case, K. E., & Mayer, C. J. (1996). Housing price dynamics within a metropolitan area. *Regional Science and Urban Economics1*, *26*, 387–407.

Cervero, R., & Landis, J. (1997). *Twenty Years of The Bay Area Rapid Transit System: Land Use And Development Impacts*. *31*(4), 309–333.

Clark, D. E., & Cosgrove, J. C. (1990). Hedonic Prices, Identification, and the Demand for Public Safety. *Journal of Regional Science*, Vol. 30, pp. 105–121. https://doi.org/10.1111/j.1467-9787.1990.tb00083.x

Clark, T. (2004). Urban Amenities: Lakes, Opera, and Juice Bars: Do They Drive Development? *Research in Urban Policy*, *9*, 103–140. Retrieved from http://uq.summon.serialssolutions.com/2.0.0/link/0/eLvHCXMwY2BQsDRLM0yzNDJPSQXWr WlJycAaz8Q4MSUxMTUpEdTiQBnrQCrN3YQYmFLzRBmU3FxDnD10YUVjfG ISqNefXFIcbwY62xDYYzAUY-BNBK0AzysB7xRLAQCS_B75%0Ahttp://www.emeraldinsight.com/books.htm?issn=1479-3520&volume=9&chapt

Cornwell, C., & Trumbull, W. N. . (1994). Estimating the Economic Model of Crime with Panel Data. *The Review of Economics and Statistics*, *76*(2), 360–366.

Cullen, J. B., & Levitt, S. D. (1999). Crime, Urban Flight, and the Consequences for Cities. *The Review of Eocnomics and Statistics*, *81*(2), 159–169. Retrieved from http://www.jstor.org/stable/2646853

de Sombre, S. (2013). *AWA 2013 - Generationenspezifische Konsumstile*. Institut für Demoskopie Allensbach.

Degen, K., & Fischer, A. M. (2017). Immigration and Swiss House Prices. *Swiss Journal of Economics and Statistics*, *153*(1), 15–36. https://doi.org/10.1016/j.tetlet.2008.08.010

Diamond, D. B., & Tolley, G. S. (1982). *The Economics of Urban Amenities* (1st ed.; E. S. Mills, Ed.). https://doi.org/10.1177/1527002503261491

Dietz, B., Enste, D. H., & Eyerund, T. (2016). Mythos Generation Y? *Roman Herzog Institut e.V.*, *28*(28), 44. Retrieved from http://www.verhaltensoekonomik.org/studien/rhi-publikationen/beitrag/bernhard-dietz-dominik-enste-theresa-eyerund-mythos-generation-y-304097

Dimock, M. (2018). Defining generations: Where Millennials end and Generation Z begins. Retrieved June 11, 2019, from Fact Tank website: https://www.pewresearch.org/fact-tank/2019/01/17/where-millennials-end-and-generation-z-begins/

Dubin, R. A. and A. C. G. (1982). Valuation ofEducation and Crime Neighborhood Characteristics through Hedonic Housing Prices. *Population and Environment*, *5*(3), 166–181.

Dugan, L. (1999). The Effect of Criminal Victimization on a Household's Moving Decision. *Criminology*, *37*(4), 903–930. https://doi.org/10.1111/j.1745-9125.1999.tb00509.x

Eide, E., Aasness, J., & Skjerpen, T. (1994). Economics of crime : deterrence and the rational offender. In *Contributions to economic analysis*. New York City: North Holland.

Eilers, L., Paloyo, A. R., & Vance, C. (2017). *Rental prices in Germany: A comparison between migrants and natives* (No. 736). Essen.

Ellen, I. G., & O'Regan, K. (2010). Crime and urban flight revisited: The effect of the 1990s drop in crime on cities. *Journal of Urban Economics*, *68*(3), 247–259. https://doi.org/10.1016/j.jue.2010.05.002

Entorf, H., & Spengler, H. (2000). Socioeconomic and demographic factors of crime in Germany. *International Review of Law and Economics*, *20*(1), 75–106. https://doi.org/10.1016/S0144-8188(00)00022-3

Eurostat. (2018). Migration and migrant population statistics. Retrieved February 1, 2019, from https://ec.europa.eu/eurostat/statistics-explained/index.php/Migration_and_migrant_population_statistics

Eurostat. (2019). Homeownership Rate European Union. Retrieved from http://appsso.eurostat.ec.europa.eu/nui/show.do?dataset=ilc_lvho02&lang=de

Fagan, J., & Freeman, R. B. (1999). Crime and Work. *Crime and Justice*, *25*(1999), 225–290.

Fischer, A. M. (2012). Immigrant language barriers and house prices. *Regional Science and Urban Economics*, *42*(3), 389–395. https://doi.org/10.1016/j.regsciurbeco.2011.11.003

Fox, J. A., & Zawitz, M. (2007). Homicide trends in the United States. https://doi.org/www.ojp.usdoj/bjs/

Frey, W. H. (1995). Immigration and Internal Migration 'Flight' from US Metropolitan Areas: Toward a New Demographic Balkanisation. *Urban Studies*, *32*(4–5), 733–757. https://doi.org/10.1080/00420989550012861

Frobenius, F. G. (1912). Über Matrizen aus nicht negativen Elementen. *Sitzung Der Physikalisch-Mathematischen Classe*, 456–477.

Fuhrich, M. (2009). Städte in Deutschland. Retrieved June 23, 2019, from BBSR - Raumordnungsprognose 2025/2050 website: https://www.bbsr.bund.de/BBSR/DE/Stadtentwicklung/StadtentwicklungDeutschland/staedte-gemeinden/projekte StaedteDeutschland/staedte.html?nn=1855822

Gat, D. (1998). Urban Focal Points and Design Quality Influence Rents: The Case of the Tel Aviv Office Market. *Journal Of Real Estate Research*, *16*(2), 229–247.

Gibbons, S. (2004). The Costs of Urban Property Crime. *The Economic Journal*, *114*(499), 441–463.

Gibbons, S., Mourato, S., & Mendes, G. (2014). *The amenity value of English nature : a hedonic price approach*. https://doi.org/10.1007/s10640-013-9664-9

Glaeser, E. L., & Gottlieb, J. D. (2006). *Urban Resugence and the Consumer City* (No. 2109). Cambridge.

Glaeser, E. L., Kahn, M. E., & Rappaport, J. (2008). Why do the poor live in cities? The role of public transportation. *Journal of Urban Economics*, *63*(1), 1–24. https://doi.org/10.1016/j.jue.2006.12.004

Glaeser, E. L., Kolko, J., & Saiz, A. (2001). Consumer city. *Journal of Economic Geography*, *1*(1), 27–50. https://doi.org/10.1093/jeg/1.1.27

González, L., & Ortega, F. (2013). Immigration and Housing Booms: Evidence from Spain. *Journal of Regional Science*, *53*(1), 37–59. https://doi.org/10.1111/jors.12010

Gray, C. M., & Joelson, M. R. (1979). Neighborhood crime and the demand for central city housing. In *The Cost of Crime* (pp. 47–60). Beverly Hills, CA: Sage.

Green, S. B. (1991). How Many Subjects Does It Take To Do A Regression Analysis, Multivariate Behavioural Research. *Multivariate Behavioral Research*, *26*(3), 499–510. https://doi.org/10.1207/s15327906mbr2603

Han, L., Bandyopadhyay, S., & Bhattacharya, S. (2013). Determinants of violent and property crimes in England and Wales: a panel data analysis. *Applied Economics*, *45*, 4820–4830. https://doi.org/10.1080/00036846.2013.806782

Ihlanfeldt, K., & Mayock, T. (2010). Panel data estimates of the effects of different types of crime on housing prices. *Regional Science and Urban Economics*, *40*(2–3), 161–172. https://doi.org/10.1016/j.regsciurbeco.2010.02.005

Jaeger, D. A., Ruist, J., & Stuhler, J. (2017). Shift-Share Instruments and the Impact of Immigration. *NBER Working Paper Series*, (24285), 55. https://doi.org/10.3386/w24285

Janko, Z., & Popli, G. (2015). This is a repository copy of Examining the Link between Crime and Unemployment: A Time Series Analysis for Canada. *Applied Economics*, *47*(37), 4007–4019. https://doi.org/10.1080/00036846.2015.1023942

Justice, P. C. on L. E. and A. of. (1967). The Challenge of Crime in a Free Society. In *United States Government Printing Office*. Washington D.C.

Kalantaryan, S. (2013). Housing Market Responses to Immigration: Evidence from Italy. In *Ssrn* (No. 83). https://doi.org/10.2139/ssrn.2377269

Kauko, T. (2006). *What makes a location attractive for the housing consumer? Preliminary findings from metropolitan Helsinki and Randstad Holland using the analytical hierarchy process*. 159–176. https://doi.org/10.1007/s10901-006-9040-y

Kauko, T. (2007). An Analysis of Housing Location Attributes in the Inner City of Budapest, Hungarym Using Expert Judgements. *International Journal of Strategic Property Management*, *11*(4), 209–225.

Kim, S., & Lee, K. O. (2018). Potential crime risk and housing market responses. *Journal of Urban Economics*, *108*, 1–17. https://doi.org/10.1016/j.jue.2018.09.001

Kristoffer, T. (2013). *The Role of Amenities in the Location Decision of Households and Firms Dissertation.*

Kürschner, K. (2017). *Immigration and Rental Prices of Residential Housing: Evidence from the Fall of the Berlin Wall.*

LaLonde, R. J., & Topel, R. H. (1991). Labor Market Adjustments to Increased Immigration. In J. M. Abowd & R. B. Freeman (Eds.), *Immigration, Trade and the Labor Market* (pp. 167–199). Retrieved from http://www.nber.org/books/abow91-1

Langworthy, R. H. (1999). Measuring what matters: A policing research Institute. *Policing Research Institute Meeting*, 224. Washington D.C.

Latif, E. (2015). Immigration and Housing Rents in Canada: A Panel Data Analysis. *Economic Issues*, *20*(1), 91–108.

Ley, D., & Tutchener, J. (2001). Immigration, Globalisation and House Prices in Canada's Gateway Cities. *Housing Studies*, *16*(2), 199–223. https://doi.org/10.1080/02673030120038483

Lynch, A. K., & Rasmussen, D. W. (2001). Measuring the impact of crime on house prices. *Applied Economics*, *33*(15), 1981–1989. https://doi.org/10.1080/00036840110021735

Mahan, B. L. (1997). *Valuing Urban Wetlands: A Property Pricing Approach* (p. 92). p. 92.

Manuel Arellano, & Olympia Bover. (1995). Another look at the instrumental variable estimation of error-components models. *Journal of Econometrics*, *68*(1), 29–51.

Maxwell Scott, E. (2000). Sample Size and Multiple Regression Analysis. *Psychological Methods*, *5*(4), 434–458.

Mazurek, J., & Perzina. (2017). On the Inconsitency of Pairwise Comparisons: An Experimental Study. *Scientifc Papers of the University of Pardubice*, *24*(41), 102–109.

Meyer, E. (2010). Love 'Em or Lose 'Em. In *Harvard Business Review* (Vol. 88). Retrieved from http://search.ebscohost.com/login.aspx?direct=true&db=bth&AN=-47194105&site=ehost-live

Mitchell, S. (2008). *American Generations: Who They Are, How They Live, What They Think* (6th ed.). New York City: New Strategist.

Morenoff, J. D., Sampson, R. J., & Raudenbush, S. (2001). Neighborhood inequality, collective efficacy, and the spatial dynamics of urban violence. *Criminology*, *39*(3), 517–558. https://doi.org/10.1111/j.1745-9125.2001.tb00932.x

Mu, E., & Making, P. D. (2015). *Understanding the Analytic Hierarchy Process*. (2012). https://doi.org/10.1007/978-3-319-33861-3

Müchler, B. (2015, September 21). In Berlin versinken Flüchtlinge im Behörden-Chaos. *Welt Online*, pp. 1–5. Retrieved from https://www.welt.de/politik/deutschland/article146663316/In-Berlin-versinken-Fluechtlinge-im-Behoerden-Chaos.html

Münz, R., & Ulrich, R. (2000). Die Ethnische und Demographische Struktur von Ausländern und Zuwanderern in Deutschland. In R. Alba, P. Schmidt, & M. Wasmer (Eds.), *Die Ethnische und Demographische Struktur von Ausländern und Zuwanderern in Deutschland* (pp. 11–55). Retrieved from http://www.gesis.org/fileadmin/upload/forschung/publikationen/gesis_reihen/Blickpunkt/5/muenz.pdf

Mussa, A., Nwaogu, U. G., & Pozo, S. (2017). Immigration and housing: A spatial econometric analysis. *Journal of Housing Economics*, *35*, 13–25. https://doi.org/10.1016/j.jhe.2017.01.002

Naroff, J. L., Hellman, D., & Skinner, D. (1980). Estimates of the Impact of Crime on Property Values. *Growth and Change*, Vol. 11, pp. 24–30. https://doi.org/10.1111/j.1468-2257.1980.tb00878.x

Nelson, J. P. (1979). Airport Noise , Location Rent , and Residential Amenities. *Journal of Environmental Economics and Management*, *6*, 320–331.

Nguyen-Hoang, P., & Yinger, J. (2011). The capitalization of school quality into house values: A review. *Journal of Housing Economics*, *20*(1), 30–48. https://doi.org/10.1016/j.jhe.2011.02.001

Nunnally, J. C., & Bernstein, I. H. (1994). *Psychometric Theory* (4th ed.). New York: McGraw-Hill Inc.

OECD. (2015). OECD Better Life Index. Retrieved from http://www.oecdbetterlife-index.org/topics/safety/

Ottaviano, G. I. P., & Peri, G. (2006). The economic value of cultural diversity: Evidence from US cities. *Journal of Economic Geography*, *6*(1), 9–44. https://doi.org/10.1093/jeg/lbi002

Pope, C. E. (1980). Patterns in burglary: An empirical examination of offense and offender characteristics. *Journal of Criminal Justice*, *8*(1), 39–51. https://doi.org/-10.1016/0047-2352(80)90058-6

Repetto, T. A. (1974). *Residential Crime*.

Ridker, R. G., & Henning, J. A. (1967). The Determinants of Residential Property Values with Special Reference to Air Pollution. *The Review of Economics and Statistics*, *49*(2), 246–257. Retrieved from http://www.jstor.org/stable/1928231

Rizzo, M. J. (1979). The Effect of Crime on Residential Rents and Property Values. *The American Economist*, *23*(1), 16–21.

Roodman, D. (2009). *How to do xtabond2 : An introduction to difference and system GMM in Stata*. (1), 86–136.

Rountree, P. W. (1998). A reexamination of the crime-fear linkage. *Journal of Research in Crime and Delinquency*, *35*(3), 341–372. https://doi.org/10.1177/0022427898035003005

Sá, F. (2015). Immigration and House Prices in the UK. *Economic Journal*, *125*(587), 1393–1424. https://doi.org/10.1111/ecoj.12158

Saaty, T. L. (1977). A Scaling Method for Priorities in Hierarchical Structures. *Journal of Mathematical Psychology*, *15*, 234–281.

Saaty, T. L. (1986). Absolute and relative measurement with the AHP.The most livable cities in the United States. *Socio-Economic Planning Sciences*, *20*(6), 327–331.

Saaty, T. L. (1999). *Fundamentals of the Analytic Network Process*.

Saaty, T. L., & Vargas, L. G. (2001). Models, Methods, Concepts & Applications of the Analytic Hierarchy Process. In *Springer Science & Business Media* (Vol. 175). https://doi.org/10.1007/978-1-4615-1665-1

Saaty, T. L., & Vargas, L. G. (2013). *Decision Making with the Analytic Network Process* (2nd ed., Vol. 195; F. S. Hillier, Ed.). https://doi.org/10.1007/978-1-4614-7279-7

Saiz, A. (2003). Room in the Kitchen for the Melting Pot: Immigration and Rental Prices. *Review of Economics and Statistics*, *85*(3), 502–521. https://doi.org/10.1162/003465303322369687

Saiz, A., & Saat. (2007). Immigration and Housing Rents in American Cities. *Journal of Urban Economics*, *61*(2), 319–344.

Saiz, A., & Wachter, S. M. (2011). Immigration and the Neighborhood. *American Economic Journal: Economic Policy*, *3*, 169–188. https://doi.org/10.1016/S0304-405X(00)00065-9

Schafer, J. A., Huebner, B. M., & Bynum, T. S. (2006). Fear of crime and criminal victimization: Gender-based contrasts. *Journal of Criminal Justice*, *34*(3), 285–301. https://doi.org/10.1016/j.jcrimjus.2006.03.003

Schelling, T. C. (1978). Micromotives and Macrobehavior. In *W. W. Norton & Company, Inc.* (1st ed.).

Schwartz, A., Susin, S., & Voicu, I. (2003). Has falling crime driven New York City's real estate boom? *Journal of Housing Research*, *14*(1), 8–10.

Sinus Institut. (2019). SINUS Milieus in Deutschland. Retrieved from https://www.sinus-institut.de/sinus-loesungen/sinus-milieus-deutschland/

So, K. S., Orazem, P. F., & Otto, D. M. (2011). The Effects of Housing Prices , Wages , and Commuting Time on Joint Residential. *American Journal of Agricultural Economics*, *83*(4), 1036–1048.

Statista. (2019). Unemployment Rate for 16 Federal States of Germany. Retrieved June 17, 2019, from https://de.statista.com/statistik/daten/studie/36651/umfrage/arbeitslosenquote-in-deutschland-nach-bundeslaendern/

Statistisches Bundesamt. (2017). Bevölkerungswanderung. Retrieved February 1, 2019, from https://www.destatis.de/DE/ZahlenFakten/GesellschaftStaat/Bevoelkerung/Wanderungen/Tabellen_/lrbev07.html; 1 Bis 1990

Statistisches Bundesamt. (2019). Persons with a migration background. Retrieved February 1, 2019, from https://www.destatis.de/EN/FactsFigures/SocietyState/Population/MigrationIntegration/Methods/MigrationBackground.html

Stillman, S., & Maré, D. C. (2012). Housing Markets and Migration: Evidence from New Zealand. In *SSRN Electronic Journal*. https://doi.org/10.2139/ssrn.1146724

Strang, G. (2003). *Lineare Algebra* (1st ed.). Heidelberg: Springer Berlin Heidelberg.

Taylor, R. B. (1995). The Impact of Crime on Communities. *Annals of the American Academy of Political Social Science*, *539*, 28–45.

Thaler, R. (1977). An econometric analysis of property crime. *Journal of Public Economics*, *8*, 37–51. Retrieved from http://faculty.chicagobooth.edu/richard.thaler/research/pdf/Econometric Analysis.pdf

Tita, G. E., Petras, T. L., & Greenbaum, R. T. (2006). Crime and Residential Choice : A Neighborhood Level Analysis of the Impact of Crime on Housing Prices. *Journal of Quantitative Criminology*, *22*, 299–317. https://doi.org/10.1007/s10940-006-9013-z

UN. (2017). International Migration Report 2017. In *Department of Economic and Social Affairs, United Nations*. https://doi.org/ST/ESA/SER.A/404

Vandell, K. D., & Lane, J. S. (1989). The Economics of Architecture and Urban Design: Some Preliminary Findings. In *Fisher Center Working Papers* (No. 89–156). Berkeley.

Vélez, M. B., Lyons, C. J., & Boursaw, B. (2012). Neighborhood Housing Investments and Violent Crime in Seattle, 1981-2007. *Criminology*, *50*(4), 1025–1056. https://doi.org/10.1111/j.1745-9125.2012.00287.x

Wakabayashi, M., & Hewings, G. J. D. (2002). *Life Cycle Changes in Consumption Behavior : Age-Specific and Regional Variations* (No. 02-T-13). Chicago, IL.

Wilson, J. (2013). *Thinking about Crime* (3rd ed.). New York: Basic Books.

Wooldridge, J. M. (2002). Econometric Analysis of Cross Section and Panel Data. *Booksgooglecom*, *58*(2), 752. https://doi.org/10.1515/humr.2003.021

Wyant, B. R. (2008). Multilevel Impacts of Perceived Incivilities and Perceptions of Crime Risk. *Journal of Research in Crime and Delinquency*, (Conklin 1975), 39–64. https://doi.org/10.1177/0022427807309440

Zhao, J. S., Lawton, B., & Longmire, D. (2015). An Examination of the Micro-Level Crime–Fear of Crime Link. *Crime and Delinquency*, *61*(1), 19–44. https://doi.org/10.1177/0011128710386203

Appendices

Appendix A

In mathematical terms, the objective is to get the nonnegative weights w_i of the criterion c_i for $i = 1$ to n. As the weights of the criteria are unknown, AHP tries to identify the relative importance of the criteria by determining the weights. The relative importance of one criterion to another is therefore determined by the ratio of the relative weight of criterion 1 with respect to criterion 2 or by w_1/w_2 as illustrated in equation 13. The matrix in Equation 14 represents all combinations of comparisons between the criteria. The resulting properties are such that all diagonal elements are unity and the reciprocal relationship of

$$a_{ij} = \frac{1}{aji} \text{ for all } i \text{ and } j. \tag{20}$$

$$A = \begin{bmatrix} w_1/w_1 & w_1/w_2 & w_1/w_3 & \cdots & w_1/w_n \\ w_2/w_1 & & & \cdots & \\ w_3/w_1 & & & \cdots & \\ \vdots & & & \cdots & \\ w_n/w_1 & & & \cdots & w_n/w_n \end{bmatrix} \tag{21}$$

The mathematical principle behind AHP is the solution of an eigenvector or eigenvalue problem. An eigenvector is a non-zero vector in a squared matrix that does not change direction when transformed by its eigenvalue. Hence, the eigenvector is a vector that has the same direction as matrix A (Strang, 2003, p. 290). Mathematically, the vector w in equation 15 is an eigenvector of the matrix A with the eigenvalue n:

$$Aw = nw \tag{22}$$

The mathematical approach behind AHP solves this eigenvalue problem and derives the eigenvalue n. However, this equation is only valid for consistent matrices. As with AHP, inconsistent matrices are more likely to emerge the more complex the decision problem gets. Hence, Saaty (1977) transforms the equation above by introducing the unknown l:

J. de Graaff, *Essays on the Impact of Urban (Dis-)Amenities on the German Real Estate Market*, Essays in Real Estate Research 18,
https://doi.org/10.1007/978-3-658-31623-5

$$Aw = lw \tag{23}$$

Any value for l that satisfies Equation 15 is an eigenvalue of the corresponding eigenvector w. According to the Perron-Frobenius[43] theorem, every positive matrix containing real numbers has a unique positive maximum eigenvalue l_{max}. In the case of perfectly consistent matrices $l_{max} = n$ but for inconsistent matrices the inconsistency is measured by $l_{max} - n$. The calculation of the eigenvector associated with l_{max} is done by taking the limit matrix to successive powers until the so-called limit matrix is reached. The limit matrix has the property that all columns are equal, and that any column contains the desired eigenvector, which represents the relative weights of the criteria. The mathematical representation is summarized in the following relationship:

$$\lim_{k \to \infty} \left(\frac{A^k e}{e^T A^k e} \right) = w_1 \tag{24}$$

where $A > 0$, e are the column sums of an n-row vector, w_1 is its principal eigenvector corresponding to the maximum eigenvalue l_1, such that $\sum_{i=1}^{n} (w_1)_i = 1$.

43 The Perron-Frobenius theorem was proven by Oskar Perron (1907) and Georg Frobenius (1912) and states that a squared matrix with positive entries has a unique largest eigenvalue. For further details see Perron (1907) and Frobenius (1912).

Table 21) Full List of Urban Amenities That Empirically Influence Housing Prices. Source: Own Illustration.

Localised Goods and Services		Source
1	restaurants	Glaeser, Kolko and Saiz (2001), Schiff (2013), Waldfogen (2008)
2	theatres	Möller (2014)
3	concert halls	Möller (2014)
4	art museums	Glaeser, Kolko and Saiz (2001)
5	museums	Glaeser and Gottlieb (2006)
6	hair salons	Möller (2014)
7	operas	Clark (2004)
8	clubs	Möller (2014)
9	bars	Möller (2014)
10	book stores	Möller (2014)
11	antique shops	Möller (2014)
12	Michelin star restaurants	Möller (2014)
13	movie theatres	Glaeser, Kolko and Saiz (2001)
14	bowling alleys	Glaeser, Kolko and Saiz (2001)
15	coffee shops	Clark (2004)
16	juice bars	Clark (2004)
17	brew pubs	Clark (2004)
18	whole-food stores	Clark (2004)
19	NFL franchise nearby	Carlino & Coulson (2004)
20	golf courses	Do & Grudnitski (1995)
Aesthetics and physical settings		
21	wetlands	Mahan et al. (2000)
22	wetlands	Wu et al. (2004)
23	open spaces	Anderson & West (2006)
24	gardens	Gibbons et al. (2011)
25	green spaces	Gibbons et al. (2011)
26	areas of water	Gibbons et al. (2011)
27	broadlevel woodland	Gibbons et al. (2011)
28	enclosed farmland	Gibbons et al. (2011)
29	freshwater and flood plain	Gibbons et al. (2011)
30	rivers	Gibbons et al. (2011)
31	national parks	Gibbons et al. (2011)
32	national trust sites	Gibbons et al. (2011)
33	daily maximum temperature	Rappaport (2007)
34	weather	Chesire & Magrini (2006)
35	ranking measure of beauty	Florida et al. (2011)
36	sport arenas	Ahlfeldt & Maenning (2012)
37	Frank Lloyd Wright buildings	Ahlfeldt & Mastro (2012)
38	heritage buildings	Ford (1989)
39	landmark buildings	Ahlfeldt & Maenning (2011)
Public Services		
40	quality of schools	Gibbons & Manchin (2008)
41	proximity of schools	Hoang & Yinger (2011)
42	low crime rate	Tita et al. (2006)
43	property crimes	Gibbons (2004)
44	violent crimes	Ihlanfeldt & Mayock (2010)
45	pollution (noise)	Nelson (1979)
Speed in terms of transportation		
46	distance to railway station	Cevertro & Landis (1995, 1997)
47	distance to cbd	Glaeser, Kahn & Rappaport (2008)
48	distance to freeway	Glaeser, Kahn & Rappaport (2008)
49	distance to airport	Libscomb (2003)
50	commuting times	Kim, Orazem, Otto (2001)
51	availability of public transportation	Glaeser, Kolko and Saiz (2001)

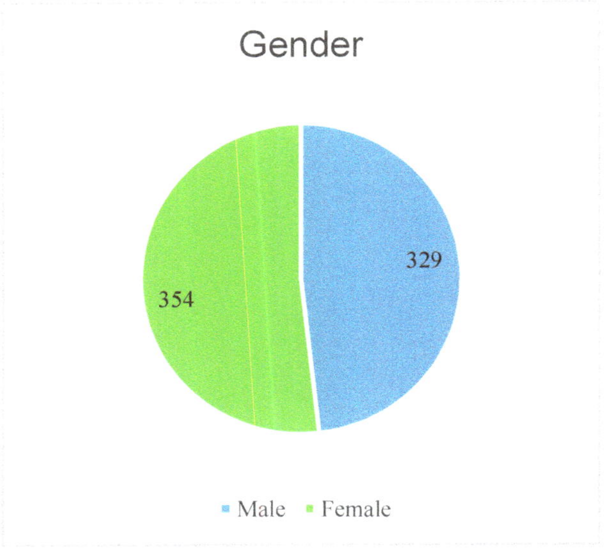

Figure 11) Quotas for the Sample Selection: Gender Distribution. Source: Own Illustration.

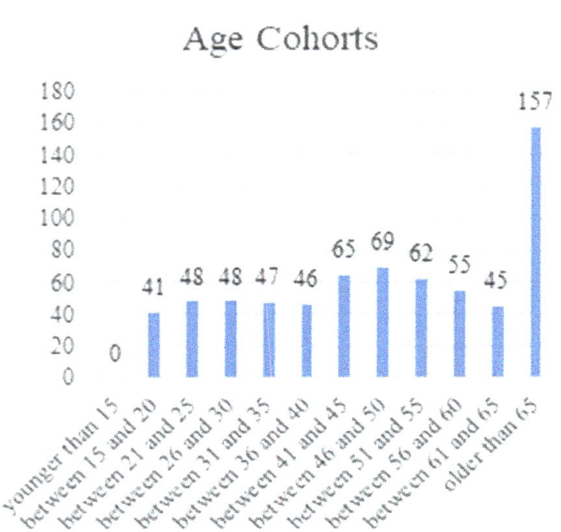

Figure 12) Quotas for the Sample Selection: Age Distribution. Source: Own Illustration.

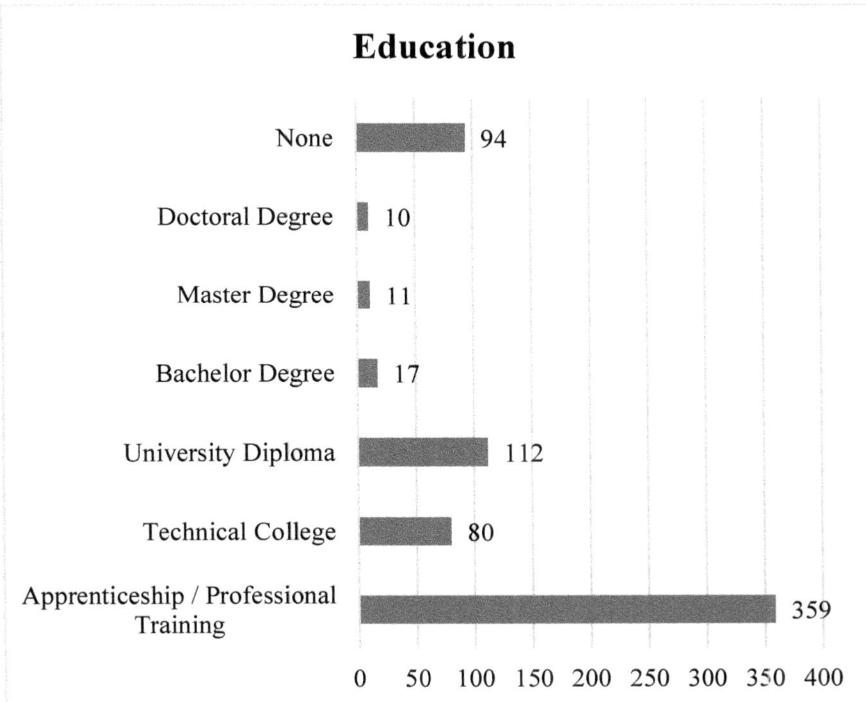

Figure 13) Quotas for the Sample Selection: Distribution According to Highest Education. Source: Own Illustration.

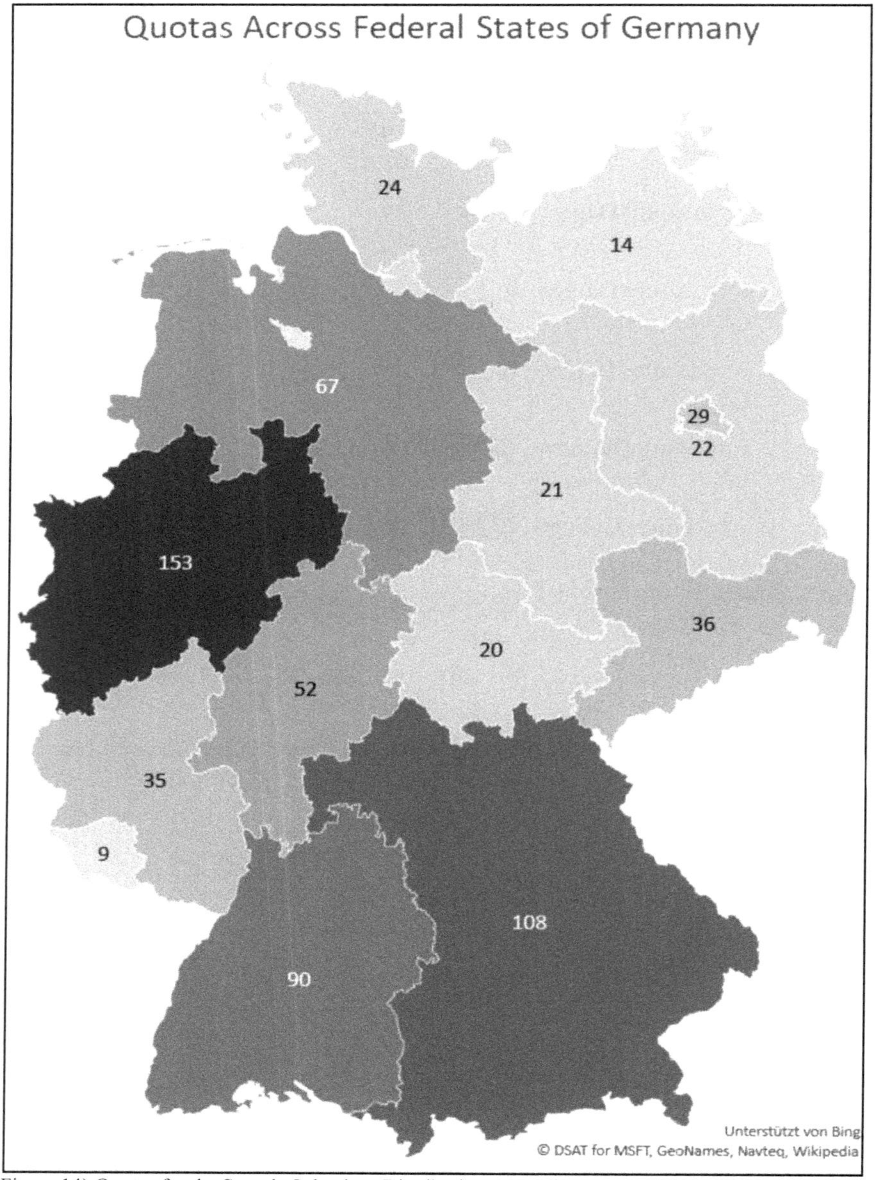

Figure 14) Quotas for the Sample Selection: Distribution According to Federal State. Source: Own Illustration.

1 Einleitung

Wo die Deutschen Wohnen Wollen

Worum geht es? Im Rahmen einer wissenschaftlichen Untersuchung zum Thema „People's Location Choice Preferences“ an der EBS Universität führen wir eine Befragung von Bewohnern Deutschlands durch, um die Bedeutung bestimmter Standortfaktoren und städtischer Annehmlichkeiten zu untersuchen.

So funktioniert's:

- Kreuzen Sie bitte bei jeder Aussage die Antwortmöglichkeit an, die am besten auf Sie zutrifft.
- Dabei gibt es keine "richtigen" oder "falschen" Antworten.
- Denken Sie bitte nicht zu lange über Ihre Antworten nach: Wir sind besonders an Ihren spontanen Antworten interessiert, da spontane Antworten oft am treffendsten sind.
- Bitte beantworten Sie alle Fragen, auch wenn Sie nicht ganz sicher sind, denn jede Frage enthält eine relative Aussage zwischen zwei bestimmten Aspekten.

Wie lange dauert's?: Sie benötigen ca. 10-15 Minuten zur Beantwortung aller Fragen.

Alle Informationen und Ergebnisse werden vollständig anonymisiert und vertraulich erhoben und ausgewertet und es werden keine personenbezogenen Daten gespeichert.

Wir danken Ihnen vielmals für Ihre Teilnahme an der Umfrage und Ihre Unterstützung!

Jan de Graaff (jan.de-graaff@myebs.de)

EBS Universität
für Wirtschaft und Recht

2 Startseite

Sie sind ...

Weiblich

Männlich

Wie alt sind Sie?

- 15 bis unter 20 Jahre
- 20 bis unter 25 Jahre
- 25 bis unter 30 Jahre
- 30 bis unter 35 Jahre
- 35 bis unter 40 Jahre
- 40 bis unter 45 Jahre
- 45 bis unter 50 Jahre
- 50 bis unter 55 Jahre
- 55 bis unter 60 Jahre
- 60 bis unter 65 Jahre 65 Jahre und mehr

Was ist Ihr höchster erreichter Bildungsabschluss?

- Keinen beruflichen Bildungsabschluss (inkl. Studenten im Erststudium)
- Lehre / Berufsausbildung (im dualen System)
- Fachschulabschluss (z.B. Meister, Techniker)
- Diplom (inkl. Lehramt, Staatsprüfung, Magister, künstlerischer Abschluss)
- Bachelor
- Master
- Promotion

In welchem Bundesland befindet sich Ihr Hauptwohnsitz?

Bitte nur 1 auswählen.

- Baden-Württemberg
- Bayern
- Berlin
- Brandenburg
- Bremen
- Hamburg
- Hessen
- Mecklenburg-Vorpommern
- Niedersachsen
- Nordrhein-Westfalen Rheinland-Pfalz
- Saarland
- Sachsen
- Sachsen-Anhalt
- Schleswig-Holstein
- Thüringen

Bitte nennen Sie die Postleitzahl Ihres aktuellen Hauptwohnsitzes (in D) und tippen Sie Ihre 5-stellige Postleitzahl ein:

Bitte nennen Sie Ihre überwiegende aktuelle Berufstätigkeit:

Ich bin...

- Schüler / Student
- Lehrling / Auszubildender
- Angestellter
- Beamter / Richter / Soldat
- Unternehmer
- selbstständig, Freiberufler
- Rentner / Pensionär / im Ruhestand
- Hausfrau / -mann
- arbeitslos / -suchend
- arbeitsunfähig
- Sonstiges

Wie viele Einwohner hat die Stadt, in der Sie wohnen? Ich wohne in einer ...

- Großstadt mit über 100.000 Einwohnern.
- Mittelstadt mit 20.000 bis 99.999 Einwohnern.
- Kleinstadt mit 5.000 bis 19.999 Einwohnern.
- Landstadt mit unter 5.000 Einwohnern

3.1 Interne Quoten

Sie wurden leider ausquotiert. Vielen Dank für die Teilnahme.

4 Szenario Erklärung – Bitte durchlesen!

Stellen Sie sich vor, Sie beschließen (z. B. arbeitsbedingt) in eine neue Stadt innerhalb Deutschlands umzuziehen. Sie sind daher auf der Suche nach einer neuen Wohnung innerhalb Ihrer aktuellen finanziellen Möglichkeiten. Neben der Wohnung selbst spielen auch die Nachbarschaft und die städtischen Annehmlichkeiten im fußläufigen Umkreis der Wohnung eine Rolle.

Im Folgenden werden Ihnen immer zwei Standortfaktoren präsentiert, die Sie gegeneinander abwägen sollen (der Fokus liegt dabei ausschließlich auf den standortspezifischen Faktoren und nicht auf den Eigenschaften der Immobilie selbst).

Die Fragestellung ist dabei immer dieselbe:

In Bezug auf die Standortwahl für Ihre neue Wohnung, welcher der beiden Standortfaktoren ist Ihnen wichtiger?

Für Ihre Bewertung haben Sie eine Vergleichs-Skala von 1 bis 9 zur Verfügung, die Sie voll ausschöpfen können. Hier ein Beispiel:

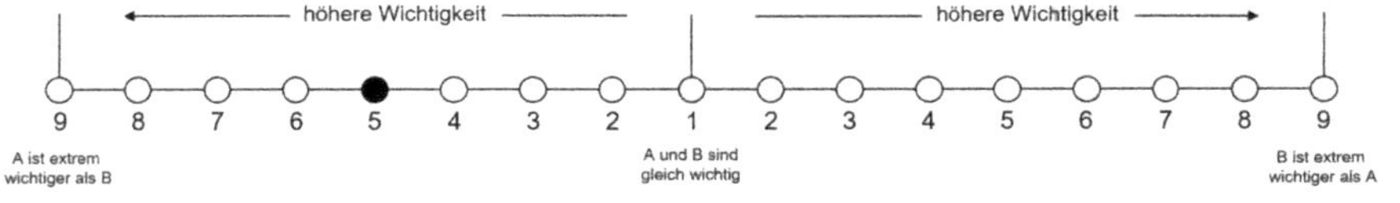

Interpretation: Der Faktor Ausgehmöglichkeiten wurde als "deutlich wichtiger" (=5) zum Faktor Distanz zum Fernverkehr bewertet.

5 Verifizierung des Verständnisses und Rückleitung zu 4 bei Verständnisproblemen.

6 Kategorien

<u>Erläuterungen:</u>

Ästhetik und physische Umgebung: z. B. Natur, Klima, Stadtbild, Architektur, etc.

Lokale Güter und Dienstleistungen: z. B. Kultur, Ausgeh-, Einkaufsmöglichkeiten, Sportstätten, etc.

Räumliche Entfernung: z. B. Distanz zum Fernbahnhof, Distanz zum Stadtzentrum, Distanz zum Arbeitsplatz, etc.

Öffentliche Dienstleistungen: z. B. Bildungseinrichtungen, Sauberkeit, Sicherheit, Qualität der öffentlichen Verwaltung, etc.

In Bezug auf die Standortwahl für Ihre neue Wohnung, welcher der beiden Faktoren ist Ihnen jeweils wichtiger?

extrem wichtiger	9 8 7 6 5 4 3 2 1 2 3 4 5 6 7 8 9	extrem wichtiger
Öffentliche Dienstleistungen	○○○○○○○○○○○○○○○○○	Ästhetik und physische Umgebung
Räumliche Entfernung	○○○○○○○○○○○○○○○○○	Ästhetik und physische Umgebung
Räumliche Entfernung	○○○○○○○○○○○○○○○○○	Öffentliche Dienstleistungen
Lokale Güter und Dienstleistungen	○○○○○○○○○○○○○○○○○	Ästhetik und physische Umgebung
Lokale Güter und Dienstleistungen	○○○○○○○○○○○○○○○○○	Öffentliche Dienstleistungen
Lokale Güter und Dienstleistungen	○○○○○○○○○○○○○○○○○	Räumliche Entfernung

7 Lokale Güter und Dienstleistungen

Erläuterungen:

Kulturelles Angebot: z.B. Museum, Theater, Konzerthalle, Oper, Galerie, Bücherei, Kino, ...

Ausgehmöglichkeiten: z.B. Restaurant, Café, Bar/Kneipe, Club, Disco, Biergarten ...

Einkaufsmöglichkeiten: z.B. Supermarkt, Einzelhandel, Boutique, Kaufhaus, Shops ...

Dienstleistungen des täglichen Bedarfs: z.B. Arzt, Schuster, Schneider, Reinigung, Frisör, Nagelstudio ...

Sportstätten: z.B. Fitness-Studio, Fußball-/ Sportplatz, Turnhalle, Sportverein, Schwimmbad ...

In Bezug auf die Standortwahl für Ihre neue Wohnung, welcher der beiden Faktoren ist Ihnen jeweils wichtiger?

extrem wichtiger	9 8 7 6 5 4 3 2 1 2 3 4 5 6 7 8 9	extrem wichtiger
Kulturelles Angebot	OOOOOOOOOOOOOOOOO	Ausgehmöglichkeiten
Kulturelles Angebot	OOOOOOOOOOOOOOOOO	Einkaufsmöglichkeiten
Kulturelles Angebot	OOOOOOOOOOOOOOOOO	Dienstleistungen des täglichen Bedarfs
Kulturelles Angebot	OOOOOOOOOOOOOOOOO	Sportstätten
Ausgehmöglichkeiten	OOOOOOOOOOOOOOOOO	Einkaufsmöglichkeiten
Ausgehmöglichkeiten	OOOOOOOOOOOOOOOOO	Dienstleistungen des täglichen Bedarfs
Ausgehmöglichkeiten	OOOOOOOOOOOOOOOOO	Sportstätten
Einkaufsmöglichkeiten	OOOOOOOOOOOOOOOOO	Dienstleistungen des täglichen Bedarfs
Einkaufsmöglichkeiten	OOOOOOOOOOOOOOOOO	Sportstätten
Dienstleistungen des täglichen Bedarfs	OOOOOOOOOOOOOOOOO	Sportstätten

8 Ästhetik und Physische Umgebung

Erläuterungen:

Natur: z.B. Park/Grünfläche, Nähe zum Fluss/Gewässer, Nähe zum Naturschutzgebiet, Nähe zum Stadtwald, Nähe zur Kleingartenanlage / Schrebergarten

Wetter / Klima: z.B. Durchschnittstemperatur, Anzahl der Regentage ...

Architektur / Stadtbild: z.B. denkmalgeschützte Gebäude, historische Gebäude, besondere/gute/schöne Architektur, Sehenswürdigkeiten ...

In Bezug auf die Standortwahl für Ihre neue Wohnung, welcher der beiden Faktoren ist Ihnen jeweils wichtiger?

	extrem wichtiger 9 8 7 6 5 4 3 2 1 2 3 4 5 6 7 8 9 extrem wichtiger	
Natur	OOOOOOOOOOOOOOOOO	Wetter / Klima
Natur	OOOOOOOOOOOOOOOOO	Architektur / Stadtbild
Wetter / Klima	OOOOOOOOOOOOOOOOO	Architektur / Stadtbild

9 Öffentliche Dienstleistungen

Erläuterungen:

Qualität der Bildungseinrichtungen: z.B. Qualität von Schulen, Kindergärten, Kindertagesstätten, Universitäten ...

Sicherheit: z.B. geringe Kriminalitätsrate, gutes Sicherheitsgefühl, positives Image des Stadtteils, wenig Vandalismus, Polizeipräsenz ...

öffentliche Sauberkeit: z.B. gepflegter öffentlicher Raum, Müllentsorgung, Verschmutzung der Gehwege, Plätze, Parks ...

Umweltschutz: z.B. gute Luftqualität, saubere Gewässer ...

Qualität der öffentlichen Verwaltung: z.B. Öffnungszeiten der Ämter, Wartezeiten bei Ämtern, Angebotsspektrum des Staates ...

In Bezug auf die Standortwahl für Ihre neue Wohnung, welcher der beiden Faktoren ist Ihnen jeweils wichtiger?

	extrem wichtiger 9 8 7 6 5 4 3 2 1 2 3 4 5 6 7 8 9 extrem wichtiger	
Qualität der Bildungseinrichtungen	OOOOOOOOOOOOOOOOO	Sicherheit
Qualität der Bildungseinrichtungen	OOOOOOOOOOOOOOOOO	Öffentliche Sauberkeit
Qualität der Bildungseinrichtungen	OOOOOOOOOOOOOOOOO	Umweltschutz
Qualität der Bildungseinrichtungen	OOOOOOOOOOOOOOOOO	Qualität der öffentlichen Verwaltung
Sicherheit	OOOOOOOOOOOOOOOOO	Öffentliche Sauberkeit
Sicherheit	OOOOOOOOOOOOOOOOO	Umweltschutz
Sicherheit	OOOOOOOOOOOOOOOOO	Qualität der öffentlichen Verwaltung
Öffentliche Sauberkeit	OOOOOOOOOOOOOOOOO	Umweltschutz
Öffentliche Sauberkeit	OOOOOOOOOOOOOOOOO	Qualität der öffentlichen Verwaltung
Umweltschutz	OOOOOOOOOOOOOOOOO	Qualität der öffentlichen Verwaltung

10 Distanz

Erläuterungen:

Anschluss an den öffentliche Nahverkehr: z.B. Nähe zur nächsten Haltestelle (Bus, U-Bahn, S-Bahn, Zug) ...

Anschluss an den Fernverkehr: z.B. Nähe zum Flughafen, Fernbahnhof (ICE), Autobahn ...

Entfernung zum Stadtzentrum: Wegzeit und Distanz zum Stadtzentrum oder Stadtteilzentrum

Entfernung zum Arbeitsplatz: Anfahrtszeit zum Arbeits-Ausbildungsplatz

In Bezug auf die Standortwahl für Ihre neue Wohnung, welcher der beiden Faktoren ist Ihnen jeweils wichtiger?

	extrem wichtiger 9 8 7 6 5 4 3 2 1 2 3 4 5 6 7 8 9 extrem wichtiger	
Anschluss an den öffentliche Nahverkehr	OOOOOOOOOOOOOOOOO	Anschluss an den Fernverkehr
Anschluss an den öffentliche Nahverkehr	OOOOOOOOOOOOOOOOO	Entfernung zum Stadtzentrum
Anschluss an den öffentliche Nahverkehr	OOOOOOOOOOOOOOOOO	Entfernung zum Arbeitsplatz
Anschluss an den Fernverkehr	OOOOOOOOOOOOOOOOO	Entfernung zum Stadtzentrum
Anschluss an den Fernverkehr	OOOOOOOOOOOOOOOOO	Entfernung zum Arbeitsplatz
Entfernung zum Stadtzentrum	OOOOOOOOOOOOOOOOO	Entfernung zum Arbeitsplatz

11 Informationen zur Person

Ich wohne ...

- ○ zur Miete.
- ○ in den eigenen vier Wänden.

Ich wohne in einem...

- ○ Single-Haushalt
- ○ Mehr-Personen-Haushalt, wir sind insgesamt ______ Personen, davon ______ Kind(er).

Wie hoch ist Ihr monatliches Haushalts-Nettoeinkommen?

- ○ unter 900 €
- ○ 900 € bis unter 1.300 €
- ○ 1.300 € bis unter 1.500 €
- ○ 1.500 € bis unter 2.000 €
- ○ 2.000 € bis unter 2.600 €

- ○ 2.600 € bis unter 3.200 €
- ○ 3.200 € bis unter 4.500 €
- ○ 4.500 € bis unter 6.000 €
- ○ 6.000 € bis unter 7.500 €
- ○ 7.500 € und mehr

Appendix B

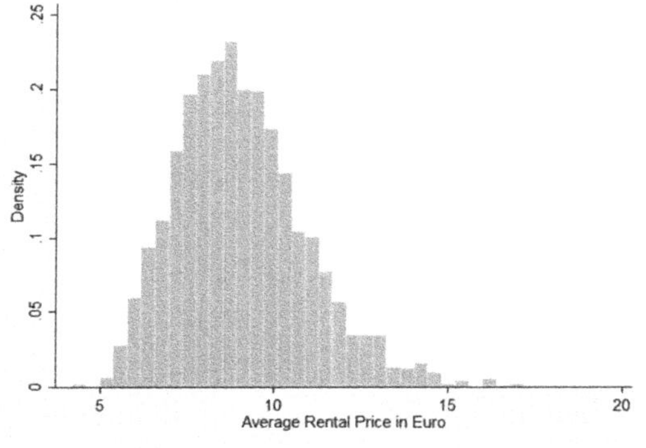

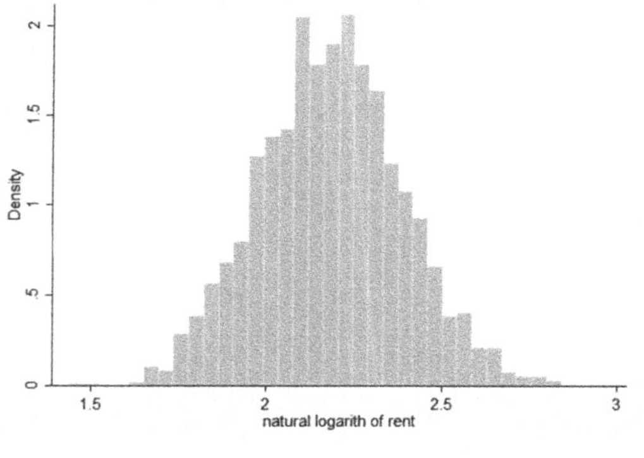

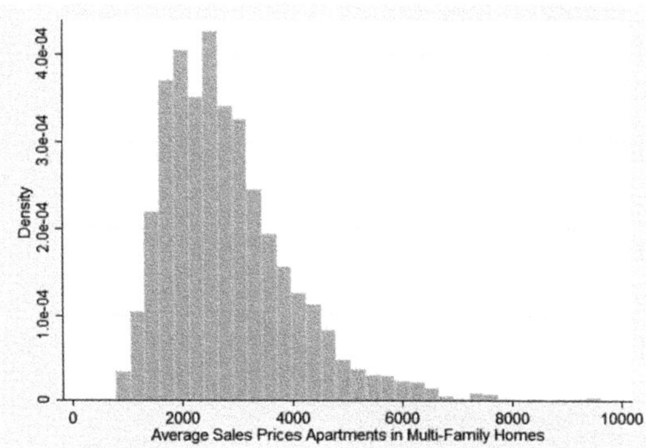
Density
0
1.0e-04
2.0e-04
3.0e-04
4.0e-04
0
2000
4000
6000
8000
10000
Average Sales Prices Apartments in Multi-Family Homes

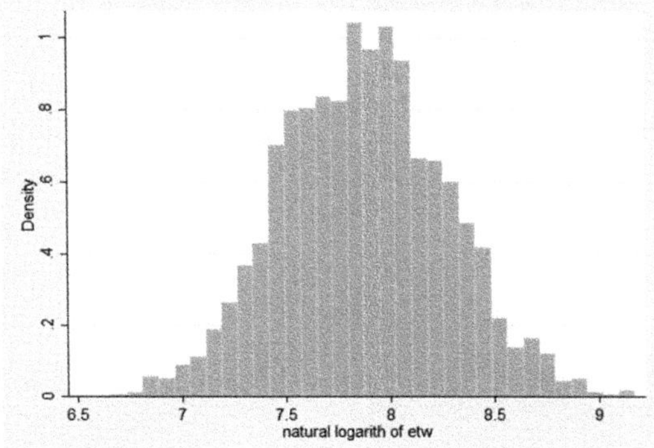
Density
0
.2
.4
.6
.8
1
6.5
7
7.5
8
8.5
9
natural logarith of etw

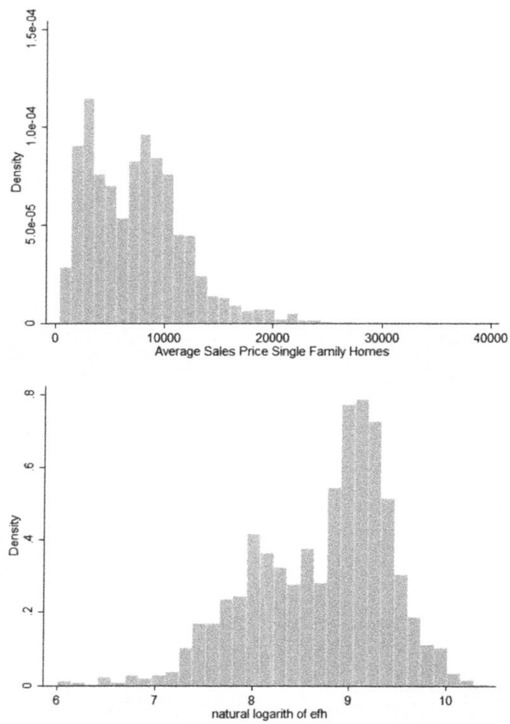

Figure 15) Average Rental Prices and Average Sales Prices of Multi-Family Homes in Berlin. Source: Own Illustration.

Table 22) Results for the Difference-in-Difference Fixed-Effects Estimation of Rental Prices on Negative Treatments. Source: Own Illustration.

	Dependent Variable: Logs of Rental Prices								
Change in %	<0	<-0.01	<-0.05	<-0.1	<-0.15	<-0.2	<-0.25	<-0.3	<-0.4
All migrants	0.020 ***	0.012 **	0.009	0.001	0.003	0.035	0.147 ***	0.147 ***	0.147 ***
share	-0.189	-0.200	-0.207	-0.216	-0.215	-0.202	-0.192	-0.192	-0.192
Arabs	0.001	0.003	0.006	0.011 **	0.011 *	0.014 *	0.007	0.014	0.001
share	-0.384	-0.364	-0.355	-0.337	-0.344	-0.351	-0.375	-0.365	-0.398
Turkish	-0.007 **	-0.009 ***	-0.009 **	-0.004	-0.006	-0.009	-0.005	0.006	-0.005
share	-4.118 ***	-4.167 ***	-4.141 ***	-3.992 ***	-3.995 ***	-3.992 ***	-3.966 ***	-3.938 ***	-3.960 ***
Polish	0.005	0.005	0.004	0.006	0.003	-0.018	-0.024 *	-0.036 **	-0.018
share	-1.727 **	-1.715 **	-1.776 **	-1.808 **	-1.922 **	-2.133 ***	-2.092 **	-2.111 **	-1.998 **
EU-13	0.007 *	0.008 *	0.012 **	0.007	0.000	0.003	0.015	0.022	-0.003
share	0.803 *	0.809 *	0.817 **	0.707 *	0.656	0.663 *	0.681 *	0.688 *	0.653 *
EU-15	0.013 ***	0.013 ***	0.013 ***	0.013 **	0.020 ***	0.008	0.014	0.018	0.015
share	3.909 ***	3.900 ***	3.821 ***	3.726 ***	3.709 ***	3.576 ***	3.577 ***	3.588 ***	3.551 ***
Soviet Union	0.000	-0.001	-0.001	-0.004	-0.001	-0.001	-0.006	-0.029 *	-0.043 **
share	0.449	0.398	0.414	0.358	0.436	0.449	0.421	0.360	0.378
Yugoslavia	-0.004	-0.004	-0.008 **	-0.011 **	-0.012 **	-0.010 *	-0.006	0.002	0.007
share	-3.020 ***	-3.032 ***	-3.187 ***	-3.232 ***	-3.204 ***	-3.103 ***	-2.962 ***	-2.820 ***	-2.778 ***
Unknown origin	0.002	0.002	0.002	-0.002	-0.006	-0.012 **	-0.012 **	-0.012 **	-0.010 *
share	2.156 ***	2.152 ***	2.162 ***	1.996 ***	1.847 ***	1.684 ***	1.760 ***	1.815 ***	1.950 ***
Others	0.011 **	0.010 **	0.016 ***	0.013	0.016	0.016	0.025	0.041	0.108 *
share	0.638	0.585	0.619	0.482	0.443	0.403	0.407	0.403	0.421
Time dummies:					*yes*				
Controls:					*yes*				

Notes: *** p<0.01; **p<0.05; *p<0.1; Table shows the results of changing population in a specific neighborhood in Berlin; dependent variable is logarithmized rental prices per sqm; fixed-effect panel regression with robust standard errors

Table 23) Results for the Difference-in-Difference Fixed-Effects Estimation of Rental Prices on Negative Treatments. Source: Own Illustration.

Dependent Variable: Logs of Apartment Prices

Change in %		<0	<-0.01	<-0.05	<-0.1	<-0.15	<-0.2	<-0.25	<-0.3	<-0.4
All migrants		0.002	0.012	0.023	-0.034	-0.025	-0.061	-0.241 ***	-0.241 ***	-0.241 ***
	share	0.033	0.051	0.058	-0.003	0.013	-0.002	-0.020	-0.020	-0.020
Arabs		0.000	-0.001	0.008	0.008	0.019	0.019	0.016	0.014	-0.031
	share	0.288	0.279	0.350	0.331	0.388	0.360	0.343	0.324	0.228
Turkish		-0.028 ***	-0.030 ***	-0.024 ***	-0.025 **	-0.023 *	-0.032 **	-0.028	-0.011	-0.007
	share	-4.556 ***	-4.697 ***	-4.446 ***	-4.201 ***	-4.089 ***	-4.061 ***	-4.000 ***	-3.938 ***	-3.928 ***
Polish		0.006	0.007	0.003	0.002	-0.007	-0.020	-0.007	-0.017	-0.034
	share	-2.242	-2.152	-2.397	-2.507	-2.667	-2.752 *	-2.605	-2.636	-2.619
EU-13		0.024 ***	0.026 ***	0.029 **	0.034 **	0.016	0.004	-0.002	-0.041	-0.053 **
	share	2.356 **	2.382 **	2.263 **	2.080 **	1.917 **	1.863 **	1.850 **	1.801 **	1.837 **
EU-15		0.021 ***	0.020 **	0.017	0.032 **	0.021	0.006	0.050	0.018	-0.011
	share	3.979 ***	3.935 ***	3.726 ***	3.803 ***	3.539 ***	3.390 ***	3.537 ***	3.411 ***	3.329 ***
Soviet Union		-0.006	-0.005	-0.007	-0.007	0.012	0.000	-0.018	-0.007	0.046
	share	-3.000 **	-2.930 **	-2.976 **	-2.870 **	-2.461 *	-2.676 **	-2.806 **	-2.703 **	-2.589 **
Yugoslavia		-0.012	-0.012	-0.018 **	-0.020 **	-0.023 **	-0.019 *	-0.011	-0.007	-0.016
	share	-4.300 ***	-4.317 ***	-4.548 ***	-4.524 ***	-4.530 ***	-4.307 ***	-4.039 ***	-3.923 ***	-3.952 ***
Unknown origin		0.010	0.006	0.009	0.003	-0.007	-0.006	-0.012	-0.013	-0.023
	share	2.196	1.969	2.113	1.846	1.409	1.505	1.400	1.423	1.448
Others		0.017 *	0.018 *	0.035 ***	0.017	0.017	0.007	-0.043	-0.034	-0.162
	share	0.596	0.577	0.714	0.311	0.240	0.170	0.091	0.129	0.080
Time dummies:						*yes*				
Controls:						*yes*				

Notes: *** p<0.01; **p<0.05; *p<0.1; Table shows the results of changing population in a specific neighborhood in Berlin, dependent variable is logarithmized apartment prices per sqm; fixed-effect panel regression with robust standard errors

Negative Changes:

The results in Table 12 show the behaviour in case of a decrease of the respective migrant groups. Analogous to the former case, we expect significant results to start above a certain threshold and continue with an increasing size in the opposite direction. This holds true for all migrant groups that show significant results except that effects are observed for different thresholds. For example, a decrease of all migrants shows significant effects for the <0% and <-0.01% threshold but for none of the thresholds above. Sample size is an issue for the above <-25% thresholds as only 10 observations are left in the treated sample.

For Arab migrants the effect starts for decreases <-10% and continues to increase until the <-20% threshold from 1.2% to 1.4%. This means that a decrease of more than 10% of Arab migrants result in a 1.2% increase in rental prices. However, it remains unclear why the effect does not continue for the thresholds above. This issue arises several times and needs further investigation as there might be other unobserved effects. Similarly, a decrease of Turkish migrants causes significant negative changes for the <0%, <-1% and <-5% thresholds but not for the thresholds above.

The same issue holds true for the EU populations. The thresholds above <-5% for the EU-13 and above <-15% for the EU-15 are not significant anymore. However, decreases in EU-13 and EU-15 populations have positive effects on the rental prices for the thresholds below. The shares are positive and significant for those two groups as well making an interpretation difficult.

For migrants from the former Soviet Union, the estimation yields effects of -2.9% and -4.2% for the <-30% and <-40% thresholds meaning that a decrease by more than 30% in migrants from the former Soviet Union decreases prices by 2.9% in the following year and a decrease by more than 40% decreases rental prices by 4.2%, which is likely to be explained by a price reaction due to a demand shock and an inelastic supply of housing. The interpretation is reasonable for the former Yugoslavian results for the thresholds of <-5%, <-10%, <-15%, and <-20% show significant results between -0.8% and -1.2%. Additionally, the shares are highly significant and negative, indicating some sort of enclave building because migrants from former Yugoslavia live on average in less expensive LORs. Hence, a decrease in demand in those enclaves would also cause prices to fall assuming inelastic supply.

The results for migrants from unknown origin are significant below the <-20% threshold. The coefficients are between -1.0% and -1.2%, which means that a decrease of this group decreases prices. The share explains that this group lives in LORs that are rather expensive because the share is positively correlated with the prices. Hence, a decrease by this group might cause a decrease in demand and therefore lower prices. For other nationalities, the relationship is the other way around and only significant for the thresholds <-0%, <-1%, <-5%, and <-40%. The coefficients increase from 1.1% to 10.8%, which is in accordance with the expectation but leave room for speculation for the reasons. As we do not know which nationalities are included in this category, an interpretation based on the socio-economic properties of this group is very difficult.

The results for migrants from unknown origin are significant below the <-20% threshold. The coefficients are between -1.0% and -1.2%, which means that a decrease of this group decreases prices. The interpretation is difficult because no information is available about this group. Only the share explains that this group lives in LORs that are rather expensive because the share is positively correlated with the prices. Hence, a decrease by this group might cause a decrease in demand and therefore lower prices. For other nationalities, the relationship is the other way around and only significant for the thresholds <-0%, <-1%, <-5%, and <-40%. The coefficients increase from 1.1% to 10.8%, which is in accordance with the expectation but leaves room for speculation for the reasons. As we do not know which nationalities are included in this category, an interpretation based on the socio-economic properties of this group is also very difficult.

The results from show the results where the LORs experience negative changes in migrants. Overall, the results point in the opposite direction of the results from Table 11. However, some groups do not show significant results such as the Arab, Polish, Unknown, and Soviet Union. The interpretation for Turkish migrants is the same as in the former case. A reduction in Turkish migrants causes prices to fall due to a demand shift in specific areas, where Turkish enclaves exist. The EU-13 results are not as clear, because the <-40% threshold indicates a negative relationship whereas the other significant thresholds indicate a positive relationship. Thus, there might be some outlier in the data because the thresholds <0% to <-10% point in the expected direction. Also, the results for the group of all migrants seems to be due to some data outliers. The coefficients for the three highest thresholds are the same, which indicates some data issue at the top range of changes.[44]

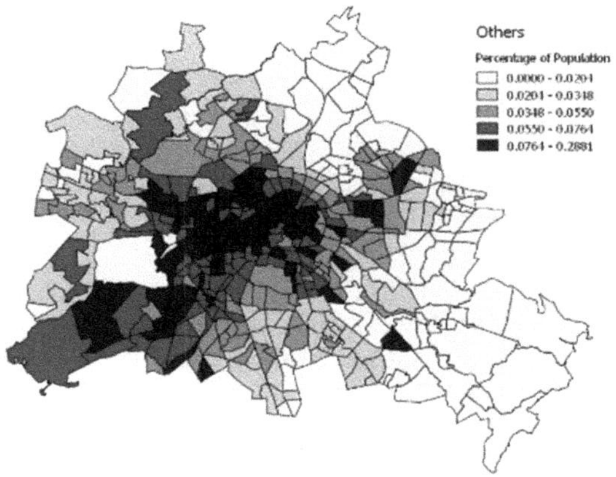

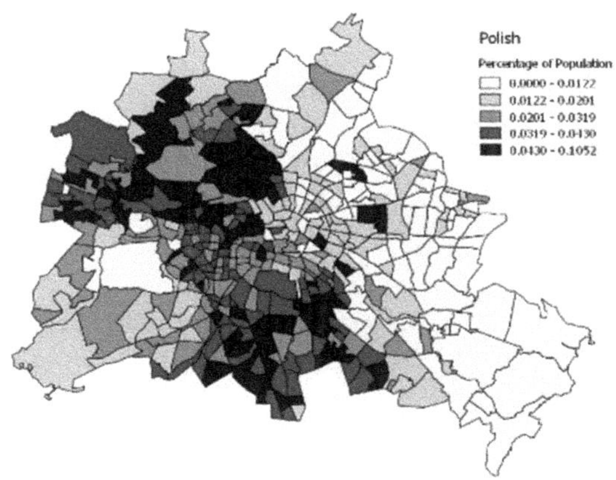

44 Indeed, the number of treated observations for the <-40% threshold is only 9.

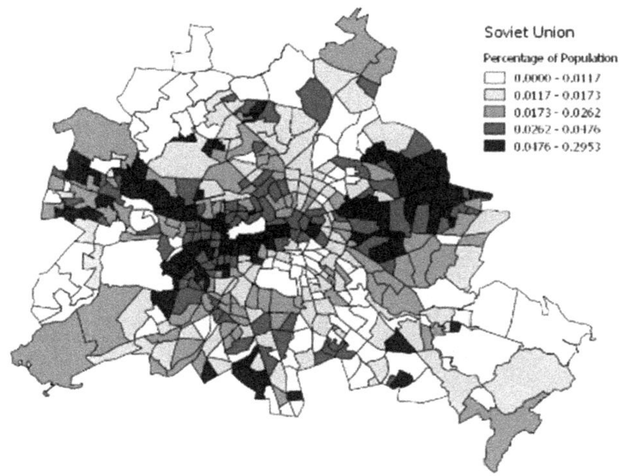
Soviet Union
Percentage of Population
0.0000 - 0.0117
0.0117 - 0.0173
0.0173 - 0.0262
0.0262 - 0.0476
0.0476 - 0.2953

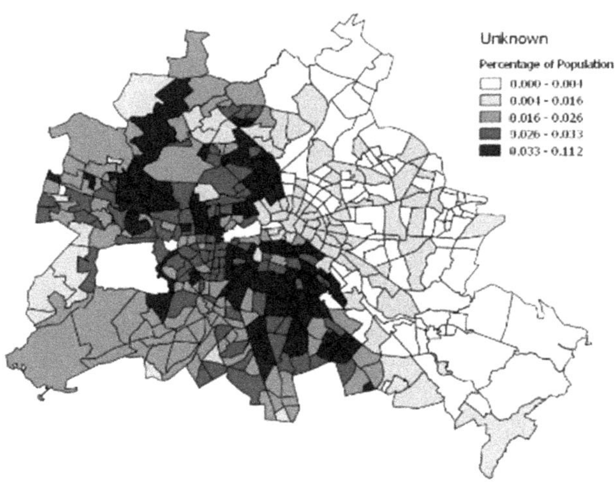
Unknown
Percentage of Population
0.000 - 0.004
0.004 - 0.016
0.016 - 0.026
0.026 - 0.033
0.033 - 0.112

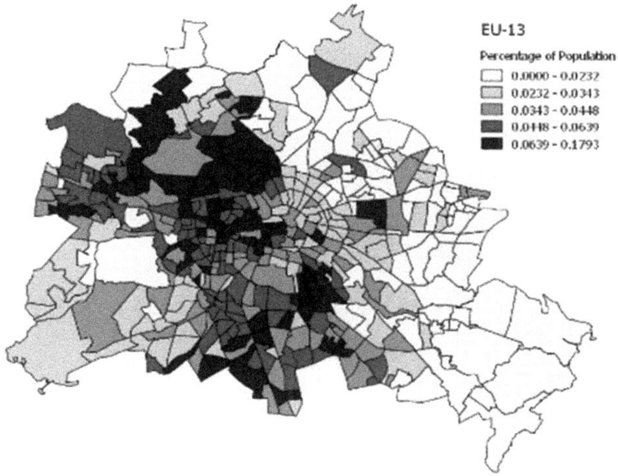
EU-13
Percentage of Population
0.0000 - 0.0232
0.0232 - 0.0343
0.0343 - 0.0448
0.0448 - 0.0639
0.0639 - 0.1793

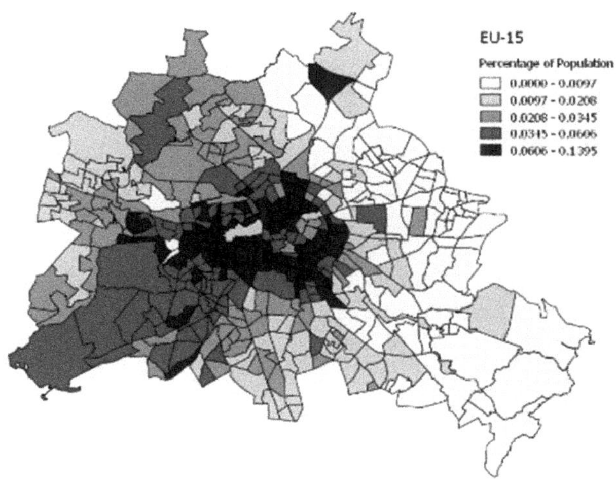
EU-15
Percentage of Population
0.0000 - 0.0097
0.0097 - 0.0208
0.0208 - 0.0345
0.0345 - 0.0606
0.0606 - 0.1395

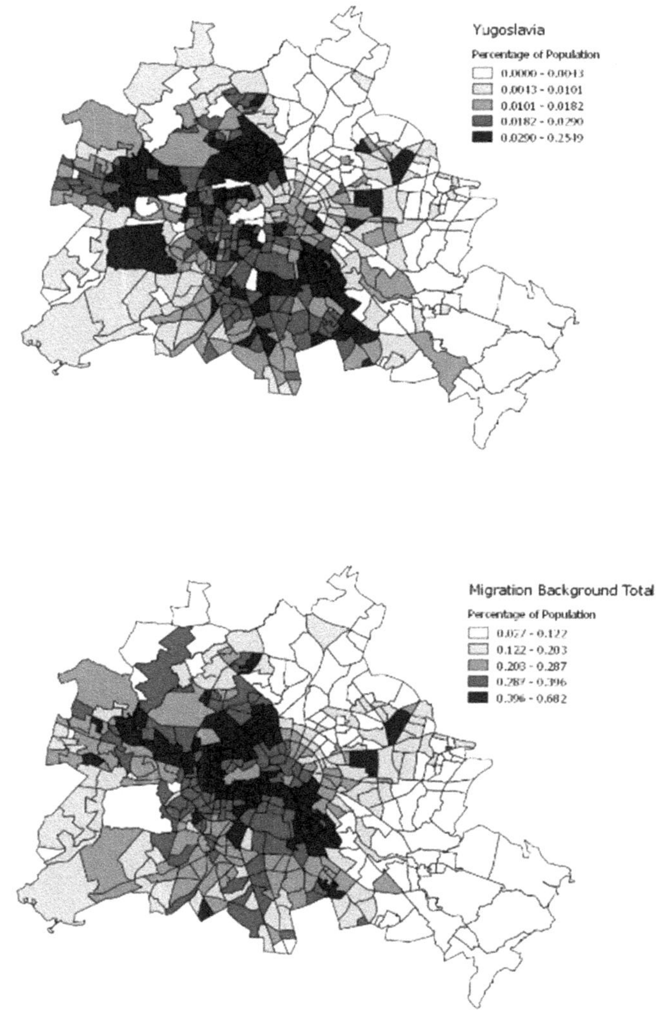

Figure 16) Spatial Distribution of Migrant Groups Across Berlin's LORs. Source: Own Illustration.

Appendix C:

Stata Codes

Table 24) Overview of Selected Stata Codes for the Specifications of the Models in Chapter 3. Source: Own Illustration.

Dependent Variable	Regression Type	Stata Code
Apartment Prices	FE	*xtreg l_hp_value_etw l(0/2).(r_violent_crime r_property_crime) $controls yearind*, fe robust*
Apartment Prices	FE	*xtreg l_hp_value_etw l(0/2).($crimes) $controls yearind*, fe robust*
Apartment Prices	DPD	*xtabond2 l(0/1).l_hp_value_etw l(0/2).(r_violent_crime r_property_crime) $controls yearind*, gmm(l.l_hp_value_etw l2.(r_violent_crime r_property_crime) $controls, collapse) iv(yearind*, eq(level)) small nolevel robust twostep artest(3)*
Apartment Prices	DPD	*xtabond2 l(0/1).l_hp_value_etw l(0/2).($crimes) $controls yearind*, gmm(l.l_hp_value_etw l2.($crimes) $controls, collapse) iv(yearind*, eq(level)) nolevel orthogonal small robust twostep artest(3)*
Single-Family Home	FE	*xtreg l_hp_value_efh l(0/2).(r_violent_crime r_property_crime) $controls yearind*, fe robust*
Single-Family Home	FE	*xtreg l_hp_value_efh l(0/2).($crimes) $controls yearind*, fe robust*
Single-	DPD	*xtabond2 l(0/1).l_hp_value_efh*

Dependent Variable	Regression Type	Stata Code
Family Home		*l(0/2).(r_violent_crime r_property_crime) $controls yearind*, gmm(l_hp_value_efh l2.(r_violent_crime r_property_crime) $controls, collapse) iv(yearind*) small nolevel orthogonal robust twostep artest(3)*
Single-Family Home	DPD	*xtabond2 l(0/1).l_hp_value_efh l(0/2).($crimes) $controls yearind*, gmm(l.(l_hp_value_efh) l2.($crimes) $controls, collapse) iv(yearind*) small nolevel orthogonal robust twostep artest(3)*

Table 25) Fixed-Effect Regression Including one lag at a Time of the Violent Crime Rate and the Property Crime Rate on Logarithms of Apartment Prices. Source: Own Illustration.

Dependent Variable	log of single family home prices			
	t-1	t-2	t-3	t-4
Violent Crime Rate				
t-1	-0.00169*			
	(0.10)			
t-2		-0.0006		
		(0.59)		
t-3			-0.0005	
			(0.71)	
t-4				0.0038
				(0.37)
Property Crime Rate				
t-1	0.0000			
	(0.95)			
t-2		-0.0004		
		(0.57)		
t-3			-0.0001	
			(0.91)	
t-4				-0.0005
				(0.50)
Controls	Yes	Yes	Yes	Yes
Time Dummies	Yes	Yes	Yes	Yes
N	180	144	108	72
R-Sq	0.788	0.763	0.755	0.661
AIC	-720.2	-604.1	-495.5	-377.9

* p<0.1, ** p<0.05, *** p<0.01; Robust standard errors

Table 26) Fixed-Effect and GMM Estimation of Aggregated Crime Densities on Logarithms of Apartment Prices and Logarithms of Single-Family Home Prices with Robust Standard Errors. Source: Own Illustration.

Dependent Variable	log of apartment prices		log of single family homes	
	Fixed-Effects	GMM	Fixed Effects	GMM
log of dependent variable				
t-1		0.5800 **		0.9890 ***
		(0.01)		(0.00)
Violent crime density				
t	-0.0002	-0.0011	-0.0005	-0.0015
	(0.65)	(0.50)	(0.60)	(0.47)
t-1	0.0001	0.0005	0.0018	0.0043
	(0.83)	(0.60)	(0.18)	(0.27)
t-2	-0.0009 *	-0.0009	0.0029 *	-0.0014
	(0.06)	(0.48)	(0.10)	(0.65)
Property crime density				
t	0.0000	0.0001	0.0000	-0.0005
	(0.80)	(0.42)	(0.93)	(0.18)
t-1	-0.0001 *	-0.0001	0.0001	0.0008
	(0.10)	(0.69)	(0.61)	(0.18)
t-2	-0.0002 **	-0.0002	-0.0001	-0.0002
	(0.02)	(0.31)	(0.35)	(0.69)
Controls	Yes	Yes	Yes	Yes
Time Dummies	Yes	Yes	Yes	Yes
N	240	180	144	108
Instruments	-	25	-	28
R^2	0.812	-	0.776	-
AR(1) (p)	-	0.013	-	0.057
AR(2) (p)	-	0.125	-	0.201
Hansen (p)	-	0.021	-	0.415
Sargan (p)	-	0.031	-	0.933

* p<0.1, ** p<0.05, *** p<0.01; Robust standard errors

Table 27) Fixed-Effect and GMM Estimation of Separate Crime Densities on Logarithms of Apartment Prices and Logarithms of Single-Family Home Prices with Robust Standard Errors. Source: Own Illustration.

Dependent Variable	log of apartment prices		log of single family homes	
	Fixed-Effects	GMM	Fixed Effects	GMM
log of dependent variable				
t-1		1.0960 ***		0.6600
		(0.00)		(0.25)
Robbery				
t	-0.0005	-0.0008	0.0050	0.0248
	(0.86)	(0.91)	(0.38)	(0.11)
t-1	-0.0005	0.0002	-0.0102	-0.0291
	(0.80)	(0.99)	(0.13)	(0.23)
t-2	-0.0010	-0.0030	-0.0142 ***	-0.0113
	(0.58)	(0.55)	(0.01)	(0.13)
Assault				
t	-0.0004	-0.0001	0.0010	-0.0028
	(0.34)	(0.97)	(0.44)	(0.72)
t-1	-0.0001	0.0007	0.0001	-0.0002
	(0.76)	(0.66)	(0.94)	(0.97)
t-2	-0.0012 **	-0.0017	0.0035 *	-0.0027
	(0.03)	(0.43)	(0.07)	(0.61)
Theft				
t	0.0001	0.0001	-0.0003	-0.0006
	(0.44)	(0.94)	(0.40)	(0.45)
t-1	-0.0002	-0.0002	0.0005	0.0011
	(0.25)	(0.85)	(0.22)	(0.51)
t-2	-0.0002	0.0002	0.0001	-0.0002
	(0.29)	(0.79)	(0.77)	(0.76)
Burglary				
t	-0.0010	0.0019	-0.0017	-0.0033
	(0.29)	(0.69)	(0.28)	(0.50)
t-1	0.0009	0.0001	-0.0029 **	-0.0044
	(0.15)	(0.99)	(0.03)	(0.39)
t-2	-0.0008	0.0017	-0.0012	-0.0015
	(0.38)	(0.57)	(0.39)	(0.53)
Car theft				
t	-0.0005	-0.0018	0.0067	-0.0036
	(0.75)	(0.85)	(0.24)	(0.88)
t-1	0.0011	0.0007	0.0099 **	0.0109
	(0.54)	(0.94)	(0.05)	(0.42)
t-2	0.0008	-0.0038	-0.0132 **	-0.0106
	(0.75)	(0.82)	(0.04)	(0.17)

Dependent Variable	log of apartment prices		log of single family homes	
	Fixed Effects	GMM	Fixed Effects	GMM
Drug consumption	0.00081	-0.0048	0.00356	0.00188
t	0.5100	0.4320	0.2730	0.7490
	(0.00)	(0.00)	(0.00)	(0.00)
t-1	0.5360	0.8840	0.4460	0.3660
	(0.00)	(0.00)	(0.01)	(0.01)
t-2	0.2110	0.9910	0.1330	0.2710
Property damage				
t	-0.0001	-0.0014	-0.0015	-0.0013
	(0.83)	(0.59)	(0.13)	(0.78)
t-1	-0.0001	0.0014	0.0011	0.0020
	(0.82)	(0.47)	(0.35)	(0.60)
t-2	0.0003	-0.0001	0.0006	0.0022
	(0.55)	(0.95)	(0.36)	(0.30)
Controls	Yes	Yes	Yes	Yes
Time Dummies	Yes	Yes	Yes	Yes
N	240	180	144	108
Instruments		40		50
R^2	0.822		0.852	
AR(1) (p)		0.051		0.133
AR(2) (p)		0.658		0.398
Hansen (p)		0.13		1
Sargan (p)		0.003		0.666

* p<0.1, ** p<0.05, *** p<0.01; Robust standard errors

Table 28) Joint Significance Tests (Joint F-Test) for Covariates in the Fixed-Effect and GMM Estimation of Aggregated Crime Measures and Separate Crime Measures. Source: Own Illustration.

	Apartment Prices		Single-Family Home Prices	
	FE	GMM	FE	GMM
Joint F-Test	0.6668	0.0000	0.3166	0.6856
Included Variables:				
violent crime rate $_{t, t-1, t-2}$				
property crime rate $_{t, t-1, t-2}$				

	Apartment Prices		Single-Family Home Prices	
	FE	GMM	FE	GMM
Joint F-Test	0.0019	0.0002	0.0000	0.0020
Included Variables:				
Robbery $_{t, t-1, t-2}$				
Assault $_{t, t-1, t-2}$				
Theft $_{t, t-1, t-2}$				
Burglary $_{t, t-1, t-2}$				
Car theft $_{t, t-1, t-2}$				
Drug consumption $_{t, t-1, t-2}$				
Property damage $_{t, t-1, t-2}$				

Table 29) Calculation of the Variance Inflation Factor (VIF) of the Separate Crime Measures. Source: Own Illustration.

Variable	VIF	1/VIF
Property Damage	12.49	0.080043
Theft	10.86	0.092096
Assault	9.67	0.103418
Drug Consumption	8.01	0.124818
Robbery	4.45	0.224549
Car Theft	4.44	0.225028
Burglary	1.04	0.963754
Mean VIF	7.28	

GPSR Compliance
The European Union's (EU) General Product Safety Regulation (GPSR) is a set of rules that requires consumer products to be safe and our obligations to ensure this.

If you have any concerns about our products, you can contact us on

ProductSafety@springernature.com

In case Publisher is established outside the EU, the EU authorized representative is:

Springer Nature Customer Service Center GmbH
Europaplatz 3
69115 Heidelberg, Germany

www.ingramcontent.com/pod-product-compliance
Ingram Content Group UK Ltd.
Pitfield, Milton Keynes, MK11 3LW, UK
UKHW021942040925
462611UK00004B/268
* 9 7 8 3 6 5 8 3 1 6 2 2 8 *